The New Guideposts Treasury of
Prayer

The New Guideposts Treasury of

Prayer

COMPILED BY THE EDITORS

Guideposts ®

Guideposts ®
CARMEL, NEW YORK

Contents

The wish to pray is a prayer in itself.
GEORGES BERNANOS

Preface

Guideposts believes in prayer.

Every issue of *Guideposts* includes not only the column "This Thing Called Prayer" but also stories that show prayer at work with life-changing results. And every Monday morning Guideposts staff meet together to pray for the requests that have come to us from readers.

The stories and articles we've selected for *The New Guideposts Treasury of Prayer* all appeared in the magazine. They involve people in all walks of life and in every kind of situation, from "ordinary" to life-threatening.

How does prayer work? None of these stories tries to explain it. What they do is show that it does work, because it brings us in contact with God—the God "who is able to do exceeding abundantly above all that we ask or think" (Ephesians 3:20). Prayer opens us to His presence and power at work for us.

A number of the selections give us pointers on how to pray, whether alone, in our families or in groups, and with what attitude. That may mean being willing to change. It may mean being honest about who we are, what we want, and what we're really feeling. It may mean giving up our own ideas or being willing to forgive the people who have wronged us.

We do know that God promises to hear us when we pray. "Before they call, I will answer; and while they are yet speaking, I will hear" (Isaiah 65:12). Sometimes that may mean we get exactly what we pray for. But sometimes God gives us unexpected answers, surprises that show He loves us and knows what we need better than we do.

We invite you not only to read about prayer and what it accomplishes, but also to put into practice what you learn. Become a pray-er, an active part of the Guideposts family.

THE EDITORS

Part One

How to Pray

Introduction

Devote yourselves to prayer.

COLOSSIANS 4:2, NIV

There is no *one* way to pray. Our prayers and our praying can be as individual as we are. But here we offer some suggestions on how to enhance one's prayer life. Whether we write letters to God, stand or kneel, pray out loud or silently, when we pray we open ourselves up to God's presence in order to receive His love and direction. So we must pray with joy, knowing that God loves us and wants the best for us.

Praying is also taking time to listen for God to speak to us and show us what we need to do, where we need to go. And when we have gotten directions, then we obey. We keep going even in the hard and difficult times. Because prayer isn't a magic wand that instantly solves our problems. We must be persistent, both in praying and in doing what God has given us to do.

"Whatever you ask in prayer, believing, you shall receive," Jesus taught us (Matthew 21:22, RSV). So our requests need to be specific, and, as you will discover, God delights to answer specific requests that we bring to Him in faith.

1.

Some Practical Suggestions

God be in my head
and in my understanding;
God be in my eyes
and in my looking;
God be in my mouth
and in my speaking;
God be in my heart
and in my thinking;
God be at my end
and at my departing.

FROM THE
OLD SARUM PRIMER
(1558)

How and When to Pray

THE EDITORS

No matter how, or when, or where we pray, God has promised to hear our prayers.

- Jeremiah stood before God to pray for his people (Jeremiah 18:20)
- Peter knelt to pray (Acts 9:40).
- Nehemiah sat down when he prayed (Nehemiah 1:4).
- Abraham prostrated himself while praying (Genesis 17:3).
- Ezekiel prayed in a loud voice (Ezekiel 11:13).
- Hannah prayed silently to the Lord (1 Samuel 1:13).
- Paul prayed and sang in the spirit (1 Corinthians 14:15).
- David prayed in the morning (Psalm 5:3).
- Isaac prayed out in his field in the evening (Genesis 24:63).
- Daniel prayed in his house three times a day (Daniel 6:10).
- Anna prayed night and day in the temple (Luke 2:37).

lay flat

For Scripture promises that "if we ask anything according to his will, he hears us. And . . . whatever we ask—we know that we have what we asked of him" (1 John 5:14–15, NIV).

Newfound Power in the Prayer Jesus Taught Us

ELAINE ST. JOHNS

One night several years ago a telephone call waked me out of a deep sleep. That was the night I began an adventure, a spiritual adventure, that goes on to this day. It involves a new, highly personal approach to the most beautiful, most familiar, most powerful prayer of all—the Lord's Prayer.

The call came about midnight. "I'm calling for Mona," said an unfamiliar voice. "Mona wanted me to tell you that Walt has had a massive heart attack. They're in an ambulance on their way to San Luis. Mona says, 'Pray for us.' "

Has it ever happened to you that, with a sudden shock, the well of prayer within you seems dry? It happened to me that night. I simply couldn't find words. All I could do was think of beautiful Mona, my closest spiritual friend, sitting beside the stricken form of her artist husband. I pictured the ambulance racing from their studio in the California coast village of Cambria to the city of San Luis Obispo thirty-five miles south.

"Pray for us," was Mona's message to me—but no prayer came.

"Help me to pray," I murmured to God. Quick as lightning some words flashed in my mind: *Pray the Lord's Prayer*. And like the echoing thunder my mind rejected them. "No use," I chided my subconscious. "I say the Lord's Prayer every day. It doesn't speak to the condition." Again the words came, more insistent, with additional emphasis: *PRAY the Lord's Prayer*.

Ah! That caught my attention. *Say* the Lord's Prayer. *Pray* the Lord's Prayer. Starting then I began to discover that there was a very real difference. That night I *prayed* His Prayer rather than simply repeating it like a child reciting the ABCs.

While I was praying, Mona and Walt were arriving at the hospital in San Luis. The prognosis for Walt was dire. Physicians, looking at a man past sixty who'd not only suffered a heart attack but had three clots in his lungs, pneumonia and a temperature of 107 degrees, believed he would not last the night.

But he did. And he lived for two years after that, fully active, then passed on quietly in his sleep. Those two years were a physical victory for Walt, but the telling point was spiritual. Walt had been a borderline agnostic. After that night, he and Mona at last shared spiritual treasure, for, she told me, "there was a complete change in his attitude toward God."

Was this coincidence or could it have been related to the power of the Lord's Prayer as I had prayed it? I had to believe the latter because, as I continued to pray it daily, the fruitage in my personal life was rich, satisfying, often unexpected. For example: An ugly tumor, scheduled for surgery, simply disappeared from my finger; it had been growing there since I slammed the finger in a car door. A financial crisis and a plaguey family squabble of some duration both evaporated without my taking thought. One afternoon when I picked up my granddaughter at school in answer to a "sick call," she was feverish, manifesting all the flu symptoms. While we drove I prayed as I was learning to do—and saw a normal child replace a sick one before my very eyes.

So how do you learn to pray the Lord's Prayer? Here are a few suggestions I offer from my own experience:

One. I found that it takes less than sixty seconds (even in church) to *say* the prayer, and anywhere from ten minutes to half an hour to *pray* it.

Two. There is no way to pray this prayer for one person or one family alone. The minute I consciously addressed "Our Father," even though my immediate concern was Walt and Mona, I was also including my family, friends, strangers, enemies—those who had "passed on" and those yet to arrive. I was praying for them as well. As I contemplated this I realized the universal intent of Christ when He gave the prayer to us.

Three. I had to be willing to be taught how to pray this prayer on a daily basis. I accepted the Holy Spirit as my guide and tried faithfully to follow the leadings that came to me. Some days I was moved to use the Bible concordance to gain understanding. In phrases like "Thy kingdom come, thy will be done," I looked up key words—*kingdom, will*—and meditated on what Jesus taught about them. Or I turned to the dictionary and looked up *forgive, debts, trespasses.* Sometimes I found myself simply praying it as a psalm of praise and adoration. But day by day, it yielded new insights.

Four. I came to recognize it as a complete prayer, nothing left out. In my newspaper days I was taught that a complete story answers the questions who, where, when, why, what. As I meditated on the Lord's Prayer, I found that it answers them all. And I found that it spoke to all conditions.

When we pray, "Thy kingdom come, thy will be done on earth as it is in heaven," we make supplication not only for our own known and unknown needs but also for the needs of His children everywhere. This, to me, was the source of those unexpected results in my own experience—the healing of my finger, my finances, my family relationships—without taking thought. The implications on a worldwide scale were overwhelming.

Five. There was something I had to do to become a clear channel for this power. "Forgive us . . . as we forgive. . . ." Forgive meant to "give up resentment against or the desire to punish; to stop being angry with." Debtors were those who I felt "owed" me something, including certain behavior, such as re-spect, affection, gratitude. Trespassers had "wronged" me in some way, violated my territory, encroached, invaded. To my surprise I found those I felt had *wronged* me fewer than those who *owed* me, but it made me aware of what I considered trespasses. I came to believe that every time I made a judgment about someone, or criticized or just plain gossiped, I was trespassing.

So I made lists and worked diligently on all the aspects of forgiveness. It hasn't been quick or easy. In fact, I find I have to keep working at it. But with the doing has come great freedom— and peace, and the release of healing into all my relationships.

Six. I found I had to come to terms with the unexpected. Although I was learning alone, I rarely felt I was praying alone. At times I actually felt I was praying with the Master and His disciples in Galilee, and they were praying with me. Or I seemed to enter into the body of prayer, beyond or above time, so to speak, of which everyone who had ever prayed these words was still a part—and the sense of unity and power in that body of prayer was awesome.

Seven. As the prayer became part of my day's consciousness, there was a bonus of grace that continued after I had finished the actual praying; an aura of pleasure and peace clung to me hour by hour. It changed my days as dramatically as though a black-and-white world had been transformed into living color. If I was tempted to let it fade, something would surface to recall me.

One day, when I was caught in a crush at a department store sale, an unlikely recollection popped into my head: Chief Justice Oliver Wendell Holmes had once said that his whole religion could be summed up in the first two words of the Lord's Prayer. Fleetingly, as I dodged a flying elbow, I wondered, *Why that thought now?* Of course! *Our Father.* As I repeated it there, I saw that these unruly people were His children, just as I was, and my panic subsided. I made my way calm and unscathed to an exit. Or, when faced with a personal crisis, I would find that magnificent affirmation *Thine is the kingdom and the power and the glory* rising to reassure me.

Less dramatically I found myself given a single word to say over and over that seemed to keep the contact open. It is a very old word, one used by Moses, by Jesus, by Paul, by all Christians today. But it had been renewed for me by my studies. It means "hearty agreement, steadfastness, truthfulness." It means "So be it! . . . So it is." It is praise, thanksgiving, blessing. Our Lord used it to close His Prayer. I would like to use it now as a benediction for all of us who attempt to *pray* His Prayer.

Amen.

Letters to God

MYREL ALLISON

My friend and I were both going through painful times. Joan (I've changed her name) was suffering in the aftermath of a child's death and I was torn up by the dissolution of a thirty-five-year marriage.

We were sitting on the glider on her screened-in porch and I'd been talking about the ups and downs of faith, how sometimes when you need God most, you feel most distant from Him. "Lately, I can't seem to concentrate on my prayers," I confessed. "I'm too scared and sorry for myself. I get caught up in feelings of unworthiness!"

A few minutes later, Joan excused herself to get iced tea for us. She came back with two tall glasses and a piece of paper with some closely written lines on it.

"Maybe you'll think I'm silly when you read this," she said, handing the sheet to me, "but I just started writing . . . and so much came out!"

"Dear God," I read, "things have been so unbearable in my life lately that sometimes I wonder if I'll ever feel like laughing again . . ."

What began as a letter of hurt and complaint to God, ended eventually as a beautiful prose-poem praising Him. In effect, Joan had found her own way to pray. "You have no idea how helpful writing that letter has been to me," she told me.

"Yes, I think I do," I replied. "And I think I know why you showed your 'prayer' to me."

Sure enough, when I myself began writing to God, putting my thoughts and feelings on paper, my feeling of intimacy with Him was strengthened. For five years I've been using this method of prayer, and I developed a guideword to help me write my letters: ACTS. Perhaps you will find this guideword useful, too (it also comes in handy when I'm unexpectedly asked to pray in a group and my mind goes blank).

A *Adoration* This is the salutation, in which you reverently acknowledge God's power, wisdom and love. It can be as simple as "Dear Heavenly Father" or as elaborate as you care to make it.

C *Confession* You ask God's forgiveness for things you've neglected to do, for things you "know better than" but do anyway—for not showing love, not being forgiving, living life selfishly. Often my list is long.

T *Thanksgiving* In this part, you can really wax poetic if you're so moved, thanking God for the gifts of nature, family, friends, health, freedom and, most of all, the gift of Jesus.

S *Supplication* The asking, petitioning part. How consoling it is to turn my troubles, and those of others, over to God, to plead for His help and know He cares!

As I read back over my notebooks filled with prayer-letters to God, I can see how I've grown, and how the Lord has been working in my life. Writing to Him helps me pull my thoughts together and keeps my mind from wandering.

Prayer letters. They're a literal way to worship God!

Free

MILDRED N. HOYER

No postage stamps for prayers we send,
  The mails do not affect them;
They go without a second's pause
  The moment we direct them.

The Prayer of Joy

CATHERINE MARSHALL

I know of a home in Washington, D.C., that used to be full of tension because of an aunt's nagging fault-finding with the children. The mother of the family did much praying about this situation—mostly that God would take away the aunt's hyper-critical attitude. Nothing at all seemed to happen as a result, except that the mother's resentment of the aunt's attitude steadily increased.

One afternoon the mother—whom I had known for many years—dropped by my home to return a borrowed book.

"I know I must look a wreck," she apologized. "I feel like a ball knocked back and forth between the children and Auntie."

In the midst of discussing her problem, I had a sudden inspiration. "You've been asking God to change your aunt's disposition, and you say she's more fault-finding than ever. So why not forget about trying to change your aunt and make the burden of your prayer simply a request that everyone in your home have fun together?"

Immediately, she seemed challenged by this new idea. "It sounds almost too simple," she said, "but will you pray with me about it right now?"

As I recall, her prayer went something like this: "Lord, I know it's Your will that we have a happy household. But there has been no gladness in us. I ask that Your joy may flow full and free into our home. Help us and Auntie to have fun together; to find new ways of pleasing each other; to rediscover laughter. Amen."

A week later my friend telephoned. She said that day by day her prayer was being abundantly answered. "The atmosphere here at home is completely different. You know this joy business is dynamite! But I still don't understand why there's such power in it."

Perhaps one of the reasons that many of us do not understand the power of joy is that we have been wrong in thinking of Jesus Christ as primarily "a man of sorrows, and acquainted with grief" (Isaiah 53:3). No man with an attitude of gloom could ever have drawn little children to Him. Only a virile man who went out to meet life with unflagging zest could have attracted rugged fishermen as His disciples. Sadness couldn't last long when a man delightedly threw away his crutches or a leper went off leaping and singing on his way to show his clean new flesh to the priest.

Certainly He knew about life's problems and disappointments. "In the world ye shall have tribulation," He promised His disciples. "But," He added, "be of good cheer; I have overcome the world" (John 16:33).

Long before Jesus' day, many of the ancient Israelites had stumbled on the truth that God's love is closely akin to joy. "A merry heart doeth good like a medicine (Proverbs 17:22). "Serve the Lord with gladness: come before his presence with singing" (Psalm 100:2).

One of Webster's definitions of joy is that of an emotion excited by the "expectation of good." I wonder if this "expectation of good" does not represent an important approach to prayer? Certainly Agnes Sanford, the Episcopal rector's wife who has had much success with prayers for healing, tells story after story in her book *The Healing Light* to illustrate this.

She first met the power of joy when her own baby had been ill for six weeks with abscessed ears. Her prayers for healing, she said later, were negated by the fear and desperation in her heart. Then, one day, a young minister called.

"I'll go upstairs and have a prayer with the baby," he offered.

Mrs. Sanford was skeptical about his prayer achieving anything that her's had not, but showed him the way to the baby's room. She said later, remembering the incident, "Light shone in the minister's eyes. I looked at him and saw his loving joyfulness, and I believed. For joy is the heavenly 'okay' of the inner life of power."

The baby promptly went to sleep. When he awoke, he was well.

There was no aspect of gloom in the young minister even though the situation might have called for a somber manner. Thus it is quite possible to find the way to pray with joy in a very serious and seemingly tragic situation.

Do we need healing? One way is to ask ourselves why we want health. Then to make a series of happy pictures in our minds of the ways we would use health.

Do we need financial help? One way of joyous prayer is to create a series of pictures in the mind of the creative way in which we would use money.

Or do we want to love? The truth is that love and joy are inseparably connected. On the negative side, when we judge or are hypercritical, when we belittle or carp, love is nowhere in sight. On the positive side, love—to be love—must have joy in it; must have goodwill; must want the best for the beloved; must want to withhold no blessing—does not even ask whether the blessings are deserved or earned.

I had this connection between love and joy dramatized for me some years ago when a woman asked my advice about her marriage. She had just had the hardest blow any feminine ego can sustain: her husband had announced that he was going to leave her.

Mrs. B. was full of harsh criticism of her husband: he never went to church; he spent little time with their children; he was unfaithful. "Only God can change him," Mrs. B. intoned, gloomily.

Having seen by then many answers to prayer as the result of combining love with joy, I suggested to Mrs. B. that she demonstrate her love by asking God to rain His blessings—spiritual, physical, and material—on her husband, then leave him to God.

It turned out that she was unwilling to pray that way. "The only thing that will ever bring him to his senses and back to God is trouble and more trouble" was her view. And her prayers fell to the ground. The husband eventually got a divorce and married someone else.

I have often wondered what would have happened if my friend had prayed for her husband with a prayer of joy. She thought that she loved her husband. Yet, in God's eyes, real love is never just a reaction to another's behavior. Love itself takes joyous initiative in creative action.

Recently, I have been pondering this principle of the power of joy in relation to world peace. Even for those who completely believe in prayer, it isn't easy to know how to pray for other nations. It's especially hard when their ideals are not ours and when we are considered enemies.

But perhaps Christ is saying to us: "The people of all nations are My children. If you are going to be true sons of My Father, you are going to have to bless them that curse you, even pray for them that despitefully use you."

Now obviously we cannot bless and pray for people who despitefully use us, or with whom we are at odds, unless our prayer has that element of just plain goodwill that lies at the heart of joy and love.

So, it may be that if even a handful of Americans could pray with that kind of joy for the people of nations such as Russia and Cuba [or Libya or Iraq; eds.]—with the expectation of good, asking for God's all-abundant blessings on them in every sphere—tremendous results would be forthcoming.

God's way is to make "his sun to rise on the evil and on the good" (Matthew 5:45), and His sun of love plus joy is the only power in the universe capable of transforming people and situations—even international ones.

How to Deepen Your Prayer Life

L. DOYLE MASTERS

If you want to deepen your prayer life, study the prayer Jesus prayed in the garden of Gethsemane (Luke 22:39–46).

As a spiritual exercise—and before reading the listing below—take a sheet of paper and jot down how this passage applies to your life.

Here are seven steps to spiritual strength contained in Christ's Gethsemane experience:

Place. Have a regular place to pray where you can feel in tune with God. Jesus "came out, and went . . . to the Mount of Olives" (Luke 22:39) (vs. 39; all quotations from the rsv).

Practice. Develop the regular practice of prayer. It really helps to have the habit. Jesus went, "as was his custom" (vs. 39).

Privacy. There are times for group prayer, but personal growth in prayer usually comes from being alone with God. Jesus "withdrew from them about a stone's throw" (vs. 41).

Posture. Pray in any position, but remember that kneeling to pray helps develop humility. Jesus "knelt down and prayed" (vs. 41).

Purpose. Forget self, seek God's will. Jesus prayed, "nevertheless not my will, but thine, be done" (vs 42).

Price. Be ready to pay the price. Real prayer is the process of emptying oneself of negatives so that God can come in with His positive good. "And being in an agony he prayed more earnestly; and his sweat became like great drops of blood falling down upon the ground" (vs. 44).

Power. Prayer brings special help and power from above. "There appeared to him an angel from heaven, strengthening him" (vs. 43).

2.

Prayer that Listens

I Was Silent

I was silent
  and I heard His voice.
I was silent
  and He heard mine.

JOAN BARLAND HENDERSON

One Life to Choose

MAXINE MONTGOMERY

I knew a lot about life on a farm by the time I was twelve, for I had spent two summers in the gaunt farmhouse of my sister Nadine—a place which smelled faintly of lye soap and smoked ham and had bees in the weatherboarding. I remember wading through dog fennel and sliding down a clay bank to the outhouse and mincing barefoot through hay-stubble carrying a burlap-wrapped jug of water to thirsty hay hands. I had smelled the fragrance of sweet clover. But I wasn't having any.

"This is not for me," I told myself. I didn't want a life like Nadine's. I didn't want to be a farmer's wife.

I wanted to be a missionary—carrying the Greatest Story to those who had not heard, teaching heathen children in a mud hut if need be. The very thought of Africa could quicken the ache in me. I rejoiced each day in my well-mapped life and resolutely repeated my early decision: I will be a missionary. Wherever God leads, I will go.

Life was pretty serene until at age nineteen I met Clifford. He came to church one day with another sister's friend. I stood on the brink of love unaware. Just one deep blue glance, and I was helpless, tripped up by my own heartstrings. *Oh, let him be a preacher, Lord!*

When I heard him sing, I was lost. "God, do something," I pleaded. "Surely this is the one You have in mind for me."

But Clifford was a farmer. And that was exactly what he wanted to be. I sounded him out carefully, sure that God or someone had made a mistake.

No, he liked to farm. His hands fitted the steering wheel of a tractor. Nothing on earth gave him a greater sense of accomplishment than seeing the earth curling black behind his plow.

Still I baited him. "Cliff," I said, "there are other lands—a hundred mountains to climb, a desert to cross, new fields to cultivate . . ."

"I like it here," he said and kissed me squarely on the nose. "But I guess you're just not the type to carry an egg bucket."

Nothing changed during the next three years while I was teaching and going to college. Cliff wanted me to marry him—and I wanted to—but couldn't.

Yet all the time, he was indoctrinating me in the lore of the farm, and there came a summer day following my third year of college when my defenses caved in. It was the day I rode with him on the little Farmall while he mowed the clover meadow. I watched the swallows circling the field for the bugs aroused by his machine, and I thought I would drown in the purpling twilight. I was visualizing myself with a baby in my arms running to greet him at the end of a day like this.

"I'll marry you, Clifford," I said that night. We had taken our soda pop out beneath the maple tree and sat gazing at the moon floating in the pond below us.

I could hear the crickets begin to sing, and then the frogs took up the rhythm. I thought he would reach out for me, but he didn't. He sat silent with his back against the tree so long I thought that perhaps he had not heard.

"Cliff," I whispered. He grasped my hand, then lifted my chin tenderly. "You know it wouldn't work," he said at last. "You don't belong on a farm."

"I won't be unhappy," I argued. "I've made up my mind."

But he shook his head. "You have to do what the Lord tells you to do. I would never forgive myself if you missed your way because of me."

"I know what I'm doing," I cried desperately, but he stood me on my feet and began walking me toward his car. And I knew he was right. How could I say to God that I wanted to go my own way?

"Lord," I cried all that night, "help me! Help me! Surely You have seen the pain in Clifford and You know the torment I have brought him. I am no longer sure of the way I should go. Lead me."

And I know that He did lead me. I had to go to the seminary; of that I was sure. I had to know beyond a shadow of doubt what God's will was for me. So I applied for a scholarship, and when it came, I said good-bye to Cliff—maybe, I thought, forever.

I plunged into seminary life with all the fervor and energy I possessed. I took over a Sunday school department in one church and a training course in another. I gulped down great quantities of Old and New Testament.

Then I began to look about me. Surely God had someone ready for me here. Maybe He had been leading me to the perfect mate all along. So I looked those preacher boys over. They were there by the hundreds. They laughed and talked and sang and preached on street corners on Friday nights and in churches on weekends. They were handsome, gifted, warm-hearted. They were my dear friends, but none of them was especially for me.

Then another thought gripped me: maybe God expected me to go it alone! The thought sent a deep pain through me—yet if that's what He wanted, I would go alone.

But one evening my best friend, Antonina, got me talking about Cliff. She must have seen the loneliness in my eyes, and I'm sure it showed. I kept seeing Clifford driving his tractor, the swallows circling it. Anyway, in the course of our conversation, she challenged my commitment. "Maybe the Lord really has something else in mind for you. Have you asked Him lately?"

"I've pounded on His door every night!" I cried.

"And have you listened for the answer? Maybe you should just relax and wait."

"Relax?" I squeaked. And then we both laughed, for suddenly I saw myself slashing my way through underbrush when all I needed to do was to walk down the open pathway.

So I began to pray, not trying to convince God that I was right, just praying quietly and in deep faith. I knew He was my loving Father. I knew He did indeed have my life plan marked out. If Clifford and his farm were a part of it, He surely would let me know.

One day when I was sick with the flu, the answer came. I had prayed joyfully, knowing that the answer was there already in the heart of God. Then I slept; and as I slept, a voice spoke softly. I turned and saw Clifford's face smiling at me and then I felt as if God were smiling on us both. Suddenly I sat up in bed. The answer was as clear as a cloudless Tuesday morning. "Yes, I must marry Cliff," I said aloud.

"The answer was there all the time," I wrote to Cliff. "All I had to do was trust God and look."

In the spring I became a farmer's wife and stood on our hilltop each morning watching Clifford's tractor and the sun rising through mists above purple hills.

It is still like that, and love an ever-new mystery to both of us. And God is here—in the turn of plow and the hum of the combine and the rattle of the hay elevator. I have watched Him walk among the sheep and cattle and laugh with our children.

Clifford and I witness together to His guiding power in our local church, and now that our children are stretching into lives of their own, I am once more a schoolteacher. "Wherever He leads me," I am still saying, and keep bumping my head on the infinite.

"What Is It You're Looking For, Captain?"

THEODORE J. THIBEAULT

When you find yourself doing a bunch of oddball things that wind up making perfect sense, you can be sure God is at work. That's what I think today. Yet back in 1986, when the peculiarities began, I had no interest in God, nor did I ever dream that God might interest Himself in me—an old barnacle of seventy, with forty years in the merchant marine behind me.

Still, who else would put the idea of taking karate lessons into my head? Karate! I hadn't thought about it since I'd taken a few lessons in a class with my young son. But that was twenty-five years ago. Now I was entering my eighth decade. Healthy, except for some deafness. Happily married. Taking care of a cat and five dogs and tending an A-to-Z vegetable garden outside of Beaumont, Texas. Why were karate lessons on my mind? That was strange enough, but I also found myself thinking about the karate teacher my son and I had gone to: Charles Brocato.

I reached for the area phone directory and began leafing through it, thinking, *He's probably not in business anymore.* But I was wrong. When I dialed the number for Beaumont Karate and Judo Studio, Brocato himself answered.

"Do you have any age limits for karate?" I asked.

"We certainly do," he said.

That seemed to close the door for me, but I went on talking, telling him that I'd once studied with him briefly. He actually remembered me. "The unsinkable Captain Thibeault with all the World War Two stories? No age limit for you," he said. "Come in and see me."

The day of my interview, I sat down in front of his desk with the oddest feeling, as if I'd come home. Odder things were about to happen.

Mr. Brocato looked me over. "I'm as strict as ever, Captain Thibeault."

I thought he was worried about my age and physical condition, so I thumped on my chest and said, "I'm in as good shape as I was twenty-five years ago. Better!"

"What is it you're looking for, Captain?"

"I guess I want to train toward my black belt," I told him lamely. To wear the black belt means you have attained the highest level of karate expertise.

Then he said the last thing I expected to hear. "Captain Thibeault, you think you want karate, but people who come to this studio now are sent here by God."

God? I blinked a couple of times. I hadn't thought about God since I'd gone off to sea as a teenager. Not even having three ships sunk under me in World War II had brought me back to the religion I'd grown up with in a devout French-Canadian family. God just wasn't real to me.

But apparently God was real to Mr. Brocato, and I didn't want to offend him. "If God sent me here, then what did He send me here *for?*" I asked.

"I teach Christian meditation along with the martial arts," Mr. Brocato replied. "I don't ask that you believe a word I say, I just want you to try it. If you do that, you'll find out what God wants of you."

I'm five feet three, and I wasn't about to argue with six feet of confidence and conviction. "I'll try it," I promised.

"If you don't want to hear about Christ," he warned, "don't come into this studio. You will only be miserable."

"I haven't been to church in forty years, but I don't mind hearing about Christ. I'm ready to learn anything you want to teach me, sir."

He laughed and said, "Be here on Tuesday night with a permission slip from your doctor."

I was. And sure enough, as Mr. Brocato taught us beginning karate techniques—how to stand, how to make a proper fist—he began talking to us about Christ's teaching: living free of hate, fear and self-importance. As we studied kicks and blocks, we also practiced relaxation techniques that would prepare us for meditation, which Mr. Brocato defined as "listening for God to speak to us." While we learned to translate karate motions into the harmonious formal movements called *katas,* Mr. Brocato was encouraging us to buy and read a Bible and to learn about Christ.

One day after a hard workout, he really surprised me. He said, "Now, gentlemen, I want to speak to you about something we all need in order to prepare for meditation. I want you all to start praying."

This class of men—young, middle-aged and me—looked at one another.

"Don't worry. I'm going to make it easy for you. If you don't have anything or anyone to pray for, pray for me. I need your prayers so I can help you better."

I was dumbfounded. Mr. Brocato is the holder of black belts in karate, judo and jujitsu. He had been an intercollegiate wrestling champion and a professional wrestler. He had college degrees in biology and mathematics. And here he was, humbly asking for prayer!

So the first prayer I uttered since my childhood was a prayer for my karate instructor. Every day I went into my den and read the Bible. I prayed and tried to meditate. That was how much respect I had for Mr. Brocato and *his* faith. But I couldn't see what it had to do with me.

I had been praying for a month or two when the savings-and-loan association that held part of my life savings went bankrupt because of poor management. I stormed around the house ranting and raving. My wife, Doris, tried to soothe me, fearing I'd rush down to the bank and start a fight. When karate night rolled around, I felt so low I almost didn't go.

Mr. Brocato noticed my mood as I entered. He took me into his office and listened as I poured out the whole story. "I didn't want to come tonight," I said, "but something *told* me to come."

Mr. Brocato nodded. "Are you starving?" he asked calmly.

"No, but I'm seventy years old. I'll never be able to make that money back."

"Well, do you have any big bills?"

"No, my house is paid for, and I have Social Security and my seaman's pension. I don't owe any bills."

"Is your wife causing you any problems about this?"

"My wife? She's been wonderful! She's worried sick that I'm going to do something rash."

"Well, then, Captain Thibeault, you're looking at this all wrong," Mr. Brocato said. "You aren't starving, your wife loves you, your bills are paid, you like this studio, and you have a new interest and new friends, and you're learning about God. You're blessed."

"But they stole from me and they're getting away with it."

Mr. Brocato said, "That's between them and God. Your problem is that God has literally had His hand on your shoulder all your life, loving you and taking care of you. And you don't seem to realize it."

I thought about what Mr. Brocato said all during the karate workout that night, and I felt better.

Then came bad news. During a medical checkup, my doctor found I had Paget's disease, an affliction of the bones mostly in older people, which in my case was causing malformation of the skull bones. The thought of deformity was depressing enough, but the real blow was what the doctor told me about my hearing. "Start learning sign language now," he said, "or learn to read lips. In a year, you'll be completely deaf."

I was too shocked to move or speak. The idea of total deafness terrified me! Once again my troubled thoughts turned to a familiar beacon—Mr. Brocato. I couldn't wait to see him and tell him how frightened I was.

"What should I do?" I asked after I'd given him the details.

He sat there a minute and looked me over. "Haven't you heard one thing I've said in class?"

I had no idea how his lectures in class applied to the fact that I was about to go deaf, but I said quickly, "Yes, sir! I've done everything you said."

He seemed exasperated with me. "Well, then," he said, "did you take it to Jesus?"

This made even less sense to me. "How, sir?"

Mr. Brocato saw that I was so beside myself, so fastened upon the idea of deafness-in-a-year, that I couldn't understand anything unless he explained it very carefully. He began, "Do you remember how I taught you to pray and to meditate?"

"Yes, sir! I work on it every day."

"Then take it to Jesus in prayer," he said.

I was so rattled I couldn't think. "What should I say to Him?" I asked.

He looked at me again and shook his head. "Say this: 'Jesus, my instructor said I have the right to come before You and ask You for help. Because You died for me. I don't want to be deaf, Jesus. Is there anything I can do to avoid it?' Then meditate. You will get an answer. *Believe!* He *will* answer you."

I looked at this man whose belief was so strong, and suddenly, as if a spark leapt between us, that same belief was humming inside *me* like electricity. *God is real. He cares about me.*

I jumped up. I said, "I believe! If you say it's so, I believe it." And I did. Totally. With every fiber.

At home, I went to my den, read my Bible and prayed. "Jesus, my instructor said it was all right for me to ask You what to do. I don't want to be deaf. Please tell me what I can do." I emptied my mind and listened the way I had been taught.

The answer was unlike anything I had ever experienced before. It was a voice, yet not a voice, and it broke over me like a wave: *Go back to your doctor.*

I sprang to my feet in excitement. I believed without the slightest doubt Jesus had answered my prayer. Immediately I called my doctor's secretary for an appointment.

The doctor was surprised to see me. "I already told you," he said. "There is nothing more I can do. Learn sign language now. In a year, you will be deaf."

I argued with him. I was convinced he had something that would help me, even if he didn't know what it was. After ten minutes of my arguing and his denying it, however, I started out the door.

My hand was on the knob when the doctor suddenly said, "Oh, by the way . . ." He looked at me strangely. "Something did come across my desk this morning." He hunted through papers. "Ah! Here it is. A new procedure is being used in cases like yours. This is about a doctor nearby who is doing it."

I knew my hearing was saved.

The new doctor, Dr. Boyd Herndon, checked me. He said I was a good candidate for surgery and he would operate on my bad ear. But he warned me that I could become totally deaf in that ear, that I could be left paralyzed on the left side of my face, and that I could lose my sense of taste.

I paid no attention. "Let's get on with it," I said.

Doris was frightened by the mention of paralysis. "Wait a minute," she said. "Let's think about this."

"God is going to restore my hearing," I told her. "After His answer I'd be a fool to doubt."

When the bandages were finally being taken off, Dr. Herndon said, "After I get the cotton out of your ear, we will test it to see how much hearing you have."

"Doctor," I said, "you don't need to test it. I can hear you right now through the cotton."

Dr. Herndon shook his head. He hurried to remove the cotton. He had me close off my good ear so that he could test the ear he had operated on. I had better hearing in my formerly bad ear than in my good ear!

What amazed my doctors and my wife more than the success of the operation was my unwavering faith that my ear was already saved. I *believed* Jesus had answered me. I didn't care about warnings of side effects, no matter how dire.

Now I knew why God had sent me to Mr. Brocato: so his conviction could kindle mine. So I could obey the first great commandment: "Thou shalt love the Lord thy God with all thy heart, and with all thy soul, and with all thy mind" (Matthew 22:37).

And I do.

The Listening Ear

AUTHOR UNKNOWN

> Be still and know
> That God is in His world.
> God speaks, but none may hear
> That voice except he have
> The listening ear.

3.

Prayer and Persistence

O Lord God,
when Thou givest to Thy servants to endeavor any
   great matter,
grant us also to know that it is not the beginning, but
   the continuing of the same until it be thoroughly
   finished which yieldeth the true glory;
through Him that for the finishing of Thy work laid
   down His life.
Amen.

SIR FRANCIS DRAKE
(c. 1543–1596)

The Most Needed Virtue

JOSEPH CALDWELL

When my mother died I wanted something that had belonged to her, but not just a memento. I wanted something I could use, so I asked my sisters and brothers if I could have her old missal, the prayer book she took with her to early mass each morning. It was more complete than the one I had. No one objected, and I collected my legacy from the top of her dresser in the upstairs bedroom.

When I got back to New York after the funeral, I looked through the old and tattered book. In it, Mother had inserted special prayers on holy cards, prayers for peace, for missionaries, for friends, for my father who had died eleven years before—a catalog of concerns that she carried with her every day to church, expressions of the faith and hope and love that seemed as much a part of her as the color of her fine brown eyes.

From that old missal, I learned something I had never known about my mother. I'd always thought that her virtues were something she'd been born with, a genetic endowment, so effortless, so pervasive had they been. I can't say I envied her easy goodness; I just took it for granted the way I took for granted the bread she baked and the clothes she sewed. Then, leafing through the missal, I came to a page that was about one-third gone.

This was obviously the page she came to most often, the one she went back to again and again. The edge was yellow and brown where her touch over the years had worn the paper to dust, obscured words and ended sentences in mid-phrase. I looked at the top of the page. It said "Prayer for Perseverance." This, then, was the secret behind her "obvious" goodness; this was the most needed virtue of all, the one that reinforced and nourished all the rest.

I had to smile. The prayer, the words, the page had been worn away by nothing more, nothing less, than perseverance itself. Her prayer, apparently, had been answered.

The Man Who Wouldn't Quit

TORIVIO ORTEGA

I had failed again. For the fifth time. I had taken the California bar exam: and for the fifth time I'd failed it. The notification had just come in the mail.

For six years the hope of becoming a lawyer—or being able to do what only an attorney could do for my fellow migrant farm workers—had been a force that drove me. But now, after my fifth failure, I'd run out of gas.

I'd already put too much into the effort—countless hours of studying; precious time stolen from my wife Elena and our two young daughters; scarce, hard-earned dollars that could have gone for things my family needed; too many days and nights of dreaming and hoping.

I sat in our kitchen with the postcard notice in my hand, feeling lower than ever before in my life.

The California bar exam is given twice a year, in February and July, and it takes as long as five months to hear whether you passed. So if a person is going to take it over again, he needs to apply for the next exam right after he finds out he failed the previous one.

Elena, as usual, was full of understanding and encouragement. "You'll just have to try again," she told me.

"No, Elena," I said, the energy and will all drained out of me, "I'm quitting. I've had it."

Then she sat beside me and reminded me of the stories I had told her, experiences out of my childhood and incidents I had witnessed as a young man, things that had influenced me to try to become a lawyer.

I had no trouble remembering them. I'd been born one of six children in a migrant farm worker's family, and for the first eighteen years of my life all I knew was the fields.

It wasn't an easy way to grow up. We chopped cotton in the most sweltering heat. We planted cauliflower in mushy thick clay that, during harvest, can add five pounds to each of your feet as you plod through the rows. I've still got scars on my hands from bucking hay, and my fingernails are still black from artichoke thorns.

Living conditions weren't good either. Sometimes our family would sleep in a single room, empty of furniture, in a labor camp barracks. At other places, we'd sleep in a tent that often had to be put up in a blinding dust storm or a driving rain. Many times we were forced to camp out in the back of my stepfather's old car.

It wasn't so much the hard life, though, that made me want to leave farm work; it was because so few people seemed to care about migrants.

I'll never forget one grower who insisted we climb up the trees in his orchard to pick dates, even though a strong wind was blowing. If someone had got hurt, it would have been just tough luck for the guy who fell.

Another time I'd gone out to dig potatoes, with a crew that included my mother, and was outraged to find out we were being paid only a dollar a day. When I questioned the grower about the pathetic pay, he laughed and said, "What are you going to do about it?"

There wasn't anything I *could* do, if I wanted a job.

For a while, I escaped all that by joining the army, twice. But each time, when my hitch was over, I drifted back to my own people. I couldn't escape from them.

After my second discharge from the Army, in 1968, Elena and I got married, and I landed a job as an aide in the Salinas branch of the Federal Office of Economic Opportunity. Most of the people I dealt with were farm workers. Knowing their plight from personal experience, it felt good when I could help someone with housing, with getting into English language classes, with trying to stabilize a family's life.

But I soon realized there was a lot I couldn't do. When a grower promised to hire so many migrants to pick grapes, then reneged after the workers had shown up for work, many of them traveling a long distance, there was nothing I could lawfully do for the workers left without jobs.

When a group of farm workers told me they didn't want to use shorthandle hoes, which played havoc with a person's back but were favored by the growers, my hands were tied.

Time and time again I saw a migrant charged with something he didn't understand because he spoke only Spanish. I saw workers get into contract disputes and lose because they didn't understand the language. And all I could do was feel angry and frustrated.

Occasionally a worker, more sophisticated than most, would seek legal advice, something he couldn't afford from a private attorney. The legal aid people were sympathetic, but because of their workload and bureaucratic pressures, they seemed unable to improve conditions for the farm workers.

I decided that the migrants needed not just a full-fledged attorney with courtroom ability. They needed someone who cared, someone who understood—as only a person who had shared their life could understand. That was why I had wanted so much to become a lawyer.

I learned that in California you don't need a college degree to get into law school. All you have to do is pass an equivalency test. So in 1974, with the encouragement and advice of Denny Powell, a Salinas attorney and friend, and the support of Elena, I took the test. I was thirty-one years old, had never been to college and had been out of high school since 1959; but I managed to pass the test and was admitted to the nearby Monterey College of Law.

Making it through law school—which I did after four hard years—was only the first big step, though, in becoming an attorney. I also had to pass the state bar exam. And that was the prospect I was now facing—again.

Finally, at Elena's insistence, I agreed to send in an application for the next exam, to be given in July, but I felt sure I'd never take it. The examination was such an ordeal that just thinking about taking it again depressed me.

I'd have to travel to the city where the exam was to be given, a considerable expense, plus pay the $125 fee for the test. It required two or three nights in a motel, since the exam usually takes three days, working from 8:00 A.M. to 5:00 P.M.

The physical and mental strain is enormous. When you take the exam, you're not allowed to bring in any materials or use the telephone. You are constantly monitored, everywhere—in your seat, in the halls, even in the bathroom. At some point during the exam, and you never know exactly when, you are fingerprinted—a further deterrent against cheating.

The pressure becomes so intense that examinees sometimes simply break down and sob into their exam papers; they just lose control.

I didn't know how to tell Elena that I was going to back out, but I knew I couldn't take it again. I became more and more anxious and confused.

One evening, about three weeks before the test, I left the house to get away for a while. I started walking around our neighborhood, hoping some fresh air would clear my head. Two blocks from home, I came to Sacred Heart Church and stopped in front of it.

Although Elena and the girls attended the church regularly, I hadn't been there in a long time. Constant study and work had kept me from going for several years. Now, when I found the front door open, I went in.

The altar was aglow with soft light and candles, and I crept into a pew at the back of the church and knelt there. I began to think about God and me. I didn't feel that He had let me down by not giving me whatever it took to become what I wanted. Rather, I had the strange feeling that I had disappointed Him by not trying to find out what He wanted for me.

As a boy, I could remember, asking forgiveness from God had always made me feel better. Trying it now, I discovered it still worked. In fact, I felt so much better immediately, I decided to ask God for another favor.

"I need You to tell me something, Lord," I said, clasping my hands in prayer. "I need some kind of sign. I need You to show me whether I should take that test again." After kneeling there for a few minutes longer, without anything happening, I tiptoed out.

The moment I walked outside into the cool, breezy night, my nose twitched at an acrid odor in the air: the smell of fertilizer blowing in from the fields. A green bean crop was being readied somewhere nearby, and the best fertilizer for green bean plants is manure. Only a farm worker would understand that smell, and that was what I smelled now.

Suddenly boyhood memories, sharp and vivid, of dark fields, cold and wet in the predawn hours, came surging back to me. One especially stood out. I could see myself again as a twelve-year-old, moving and stooping in the long rows of beets, working with my parents and brothers and sisters, among other families like us, weeding beets.

We'd begun at six in the morning, when there was a heavy dew on the crops. Within a half hour, I was soaked up to the armpits, freezing cold, and praying for the sun to come up.

"Ma," I said to my mother, who was working alongside me. "Ma, I've had it. I'm going to the car to warm up."

Ma was wet and cold, too, but she wasn't about to stop. To do so would break an unwritten code among migrants. "You don't quit," Ma said, grabbing my arm and sending me back to the

beets with a shove. "You don't quit any job till that job's done."
I went back to work.

I remembered her determination now. If I really wanted to do
something for the farm workers, I had to take that bar exam
again—and keep taking it, until I passed. I couldn't quit until the
job was done.

"Thank You, Lord," I said, smiling into the darkness.

There was more. Over the next week I continued to ask God
for direction. And I got the strongest feeling that I ought to bone
up on the law of real property especially, an area I'd had problems with before. I made up my mind I would know it cold, even
at the risk of doing poorly in other areas.

With one week remaining before the exam, I somehow knew
I had studied enough. Previously I had crammed right up to the
final minute, never giving my brain a chance to relax. As a result,
I always felt tense and jumpy going into the examination.

Finally, I got an urge to take Elena and the girls with me to
Santa Clara, where the exam was to be given. I had never done
that before. I hadn't wanted to be distracted, and I hadn't felt I
could afford it. Now I didn't care what it cost; they had sacrificed
so much for me. And, I felt I needed them.

On the evening before the first day of the exam, the four of us
gathered in our motel room. Marie Elena, our twelve-year-old,
announced that they had gifts for me. Pulling a crazy little plastic
doll with goofy red hair out from behind her back, Maria Elena
told me, "This is to loosen you up, Daddy."

From Katerina, our nine-year-old, I got a four-leaf clover: "For
luck, Daddy," she said.

After giving me a big hug, Elena pressed her communion
medal into my palm. "For hope," she said tenderly. Tomorrow,
I'd be ready.

As with the five other exams, it was hard to tell afterward how
I'd done. One thing, though, did give me a lift: there had been
questions on real property law, and I knew the answers to all of
them.

Then followed five months of waiting for the results, a time of
agony. In December, at last, I got my notice. Hallelujah, I passed!

On December 19, 1980, I was admitted to the California Bar.
My mother, Elena, the girls and several of our friends came to be
with me at the swearing-in ceremony, and I'll bet there wasn't a
dry eye in the place.

Three days later I was at work at my new job—as an attorney

in the county public defender's office—when a migrant farm worker named Luis was ushered into my office.

Luis, who did not speak English, said he had been charged with vandalism. He didn't do it, he assured me, because he was picking onions at the time. I believed him.

His face weathered and lined from a lifetime in the fields, Luis looked at me sadly and asked in Spanish. "Can you help me?"

I took his hand and gave him the answer we both wanted to hear: "Si."

Prayer

BENEDICT OF NURSIA (480–c. 547)

O gracious and holy Father,
give us wisdom to perceive Thee,
intelligence to understand Thee,
diligence to seek Thee,
patience to wait for Thee,
eyes to behold Thee,
a heart to meditate upon Thee,
and a life to proclaim Thee;
through the power of the Spirit
of Jesus Christ our Lord.

A David for Today

GRACE RULISON

"David can't learn," the teacher said, tapping a pencil on the desktop in front of her. "He tries hard enough, but I see no alternative but that you take him out of school. I'm sorry."

It was late autumn, 1949. I nodded in silence, my eyes roving along the rows of kindergarten desks. Which one, I wondered, was David's? How would I tell my son he wouldn't be coming back to it?

At eight years of age, David had tried kindergarten three times but had never lasted more than three months. He was only an infant when we noticed something different about our firstborn. He didn't walk or talk as early as other kids. The doctors told us the umbilical cord had been wrapped around David's neck at birth and had cut off his oxygen supply. "His brain damage is severe," explained one doctor. "He'll never assume his own personal care."

Yet as David grew, I couldn't get over a strong sense that his situation was not hopeless. Physically he was learning to take care of his personal needs. Maybe, just maybe, he could overcome some of his mental shortcomings too.

So for several years my husband, Everett, and I sent David to school, and the school sent David back home.

Standing that day in David's classroom, I wondered if I had been wrong to think David could learn. Was I living in a land of dreams, a land where underdogs could win the day and little boys could slay giants as another David, with a slingshot, had slain Goliath? All I knew was that my hope was almost gone.

We talked to the school psychologist. "Mr. and Mrs. Rulison," he said, "I suggest that you arrange custodial care for your son in a state institution for the mentally retarded. In David's case, it's the only thing you can do."

Grimly we drove to the institution for a visit. We walked through the long halls, passing a white-uniformed woman leading a line of boys David's age to the bathroom. The sight tore at my heart. At once, the conviction that David could learn came surging back. "David doesn't belong here," I blurted, wondering where such knowledge came from.

Even though it was expensive and we had four other children to raise, Everett and I found a private boarding school in another city that would take David in and try to teach him.

As I packed David's belongings, he tugged at my sleeve. "Mom, why do I have to go away?"

"So you can have a chance to learn, David. Don't you want to read?"

His nod was vigorous. More than anything, David wanted to learn to read. To count, to name the colors of the rainbow, to tell time. I thought of him, staring at the face of our kitchen clock, trying to decipher its complexity of numbers and moving hands. How my son wanted to learn, to understand! And, I thought, how the rest of us take the joy of learning for granted.

Meanwhile, problems were developing in my own life. A series of physical symptoms cropped up that no one could diagnose. When doctors finally discovered the problem, I heard one of them tell Everett, "I'm afraid it's too late." I was admitted to the hospital in the last stages of intestinal cancer.

Clutching my husband's hand, I lay in bed. What would become of my family? What would happen to David? Our minister appeared at my bedside. "Grace, you have a ring of prayer around you," he said. Those words fell around me like a life preserver.

In the days that followed, I felt buoyed up by God's love, filled with hope that I could beat the cancer. Resting on that "ring of prayer," I let go, placing my life in God's hands. Slowly, I began to get well, and eventually I went back home to a normal life.

But the medical bills had mounted and we could no longer keep David at the private school. At home, I struggled to teach him myself. Each morning he'd follow his brothers and sisters to the school bus, then shuffle back up the drive, kicking a rock. Inside, he'd sit on the edge of his chair, impatient for his lesson to begin.

"What's this?" I'd ask, pointing to a word.

Hunched forward, he'd study the letters the same way he studied the kitchen clock, his little boy's face scrunched with effort—but it was no use.

"I don't know," he'd whisper.

I'd take him in my arms, feeling his small body nestled against mine, and try not to give in to despair.

A *ring of prayer*. When I'd faced my own death, hadn't that been my strongest weapon? Leaning back onto a circle of trust and giving my plight to God had saved my life. Could it save David's too?

I smoothed back the brown hair on my son's forehead and let go, trusting God to help David as He'd helped me: in His own time, in His own way. I explained to David that he needed to pray, to trust God. Together, we would accept what David couldn't do, and thank God for what he could do.

That year, special education started in the schools, making it possible for David to return to the classroom. It was there that a kind man named Mr. Mercer came into his life. Mr. Mercer was the school custodian. David, whose social skills were never in question, made a habit of stopping by the janitor's closet for a visit after school.

"Can you tell time?" David asked one day.

"Why, sure," said Mr. Mercer. "Can you?" David shook his head. The next day, Mr. Mercer was waiting with a "learning clock."

Every day after school, he spent time with David, patiently and carefully working with him. Again and again, for months, he'd hold up the clock and ask David, "What time is it?" Mr. Mercer was never discouraged when David couldn't answer, and he wouldn't let David get discouraged either. "You'll get it, son," he'd say. "Let's try again."

Then one day David came running home from school, pointed at the kitchen clock, and almost shouted, "It's a quarter to four!"

And so it was.

It was David's first real breakthrough into learning, and he was so proud! He'd go around telling perfect strangers the time of day. I bought him a watch, which I taught him to wind. Every night, carefully, he'd take it off and lay it right by his pillow.

The ring of prayer—it was holding David up.

As David grew into his teens, his hunger to learn seemed bottomless. But at seventeen, no longer eligible for special education, he still could not recognize more than a few words. He was wonderful, though, at telling time.

He got a job as a hospital dishwasher, but evenings and weekends were torture—dark stretches of boredom, loneliness and depression. I would hear him in his room: "God, send someone to help me. Please help me to read, help me to learn."

One by one, David's brothers and sisters married and left home. "Will I get married?" he'd ask. He was so full of love that I ached at his question. As I gently tried to explain that marriage wouldn't likely be part of his future, he would grow quiet. "Why did I have to have brain damage?" he'd ask. "Why?"

One Sunday morning after services, I stood talking with one of the women in our church. Before I knew it, I was telling her how eager my mentally handicapped son was to learn, but that he seemed incapable.

"You should hear him pray for help," I told her. "Afterward he waits for something, anything. It's agonizing. Here he is, well past twenty, and he can't get beyond a first-grade level." Evelyn Hoeldtke listened quietly, until finally I said, "I'm running on so about David . . ."

She smiled. "I'm a retired schoolteacher. Maybe I can help somehow."

Soon after, Evelyn came up to David and me at church. "I'd like to tutor you, David," she said. "It's time to get on with your education." I noticed David's chin quiver a bit, but above it was just about the widest grin I'd ever seen.

Every Saturday I drove David to Evelyn's house for his lesson. They started with a first-grade reader, a numbers book and a social studies workbook. After each session David's shirt was sweat-soaked with effort. But his effort always outweighed his progress.

David never let up, not once. And neither did this remarkable woman, who refused pay, saying simply that David needed her help. No longer were evenings and weekends awful for David; he spent them poring over his books. One night as he tried for the thousandth time to piece together the words on a page, his face lit up. "The cat ran up the tree," he said out loud. He looked at me, his face shining. *"The cat ran up the tree!"* I had never heard such beautiful words.

Almost immediately David started to recognize and spell hundreds of words. Suddenly he was reciting rhymes, taking measurements, multiplying by two, using a calculator. His progress was astonishing. Once again I overheard him praying. "God, You are so good to me." The very same prayer was in my heart too.

David's world came alive. He blossomed with a new confidence, becoming a church usher, joining a bicycle club, cycling with his new friends on trips. At the hospital, he was allowed to put up the pantry stock since he could read almost all the labels. That pleased him to no end. One day I opened the hospital newspaper to see David's picture with a caption that read, "Employee of the Month." I could not quit staring at it.

One evening after work he waltzed through the door and said, "Mom, I found a friend."

"Who is he?" I asked.

David grinned. *"Her* name is Caryn, and she accepts me just like I am."

I looked at him, speechless, as he bubbled over with the news. "I met her at the bicycle rack at the mall. I told her my name and asked her to go to the movies. She said yes."

Was this just David's wishful thinking? The following week, sure enough, a lovely young woman arrived at our door. She'd come to pick up David, she said.

Caryn was a store clerk in her mid twenties, studying nights at the University of South Florida to become a social worker. Full of warmth and a special kind of maturity, she befriended David. Not once did I see her embarrassed by his childlike ways.

Eighteen months after they met, David bicycled down to the jewelry store and bought a diamond ring, arranging to pay a bit each month from his dishwasher's salary. "I'm going to ask Caryn to marry me," he announced, showing me the sparkling jewel.

I bit my lip, knowing what a terrible disappointment he was in for. But I couldn't bring myself to dash his enthusiasm.

When Caryn brought him home after their next date, I looked at her finger—and caught my breath. She was wearing his ring! "She said yes!" David was shouting.

When we had a moment alone, I looked into Caryn's eyes. "You know David's limitations," I said. "Are you sure?"

"We *all* have limitations," said Caryn. "David and I are in love, and we have a lot to give to each other." After that I had no more doubts. They were married in St. Paul's Lutheran Church in a big, beautiful wedding.

That was several years ago, and today they happily share each other's lives. They studied together until David passed his driver's license test. Now, with his own truck, he supplements his hospital salary with an aluminum-can recycling business that he started himself.

I know I sound like the proud mother, but I can't help marveling at my son. He has pushed himself far beyond anyone's expectations. Just seeing how far he's come gives me strength to face my own toughest problems. For he never stopped fighting, and he never stopped believing that God would help him. There is a ring of prayer that will help you fight the stiffest odds. If you let go and trust your situation to God, He will help you—in His own time and His own way—to overcome what can be changed and to accept what cannot.

The other day, David parked his brand-new truck outside my house and bounded through the door. "It's a quarter to six," he said, with a look at the old kitchen clock. And thinking of the little boy who'd struggled so hard to read that clock, I smiled.

This David had taken on his own Goliath, and won.

"I'm a Firm Believer in Prayer"

JOCELYN M. BRADLEY

When my father, Claude Bradley, tried to get out of bed that morning, his legs and feet felt as if they were still asleep. Soon the numbness began spreading through the rest of his body. My mother summoned help, and Dad was driven to the hospital.

Dad's condition finally was diagnosed as a severe stroke. "This was a bad one, Mr. Bradley," his doctor said. "You'll probably never walk again."

But the doctors didn't know my father. Dad returned home, began exercising and in three days regained use of the right half of his body and his left arm. He bought crutches and began a grueling therapy program. Three months later, having regained the use of his left leg, he threw away his crutches and switched to a walking cane. In two weeks the cane, too, was discarded. His gait may be slow, and permanent paralysis in his left foot causes a limp, but Dad walks on his own!

When his baffled doctors asked "How?" Dad didn't mince words. "I'm a firm believer in prayer. I did all I could on my own, and I asked God to do the rest. And, gentlemen, as you can see, I did my part and He did His, and here I am."

Prayer

THOMAS AQUINAS (1225–1274)

Give me, O Lord, a steadfast heart,
    which no unworthy affection may drag downwards;
give me an unconquered heart,
    which no tribulation can wear out;
give me an upright heart,
    which no unworthy purpose may tempt aside.

4.

Prayer That's Specific

A Prayer

Give me a good digestion, Lord,
  And also something to digest;
But when and how that something comes
  I leave to Thee, Who knowest best.

Give me a healthy body, Lord;
  Give me the sense to keep it so;
Also a heart that is not bored
  Whatever work I have to do.

Give me a healthy mind, Good Lord,
  That finds the good that dodges sight:
And, seeing sin, is not appalled,
  But seeks a way to put it right.

. . .

Give me a sense of humour, Lord,
  Give me the power to see a joke,
To get some happiness from life
  And pass it on to other folk.

                THOMAS HENRY BASIL WEBB
                        (1898–1917)

A Black-Cat Tale

BARBARA BILLINGSLEY MOHLER

Sometimes, as the saying goes, there's the last straw. And then sometimes there's . . . the last *cat!* The time of the last cat had come to our household. Our latest house cat, Pajamas, had disappeared, and when it became clear that he'd never return, I said to my two youngest children, "That's it, kids. No replacement. No more cats."

Now, my declaration may have seemed coldhearted, but I felt I had good grounds. Cats had brought me nothing but trials. Judy . . . Bounce . . . Little Angel . . . Quigley . . . Duffy. I was tired of the whole thing. As a single parent with young children, I had enough to worry about. I didn't need to be dashing to the grocery store for pet food . . . combing the area at midnight for another wayward tabby. I'd had it. No more cats!

Well, I repeated my declaration until I was nearly blue in the face, and still my Sherman, then ten, and Ginger, seven, wouldn't give up their hopes. A month went by and they never failed to make me aware of whose cats in the area had had kittens. And it appeared that practically *every* family had kittens to spare.

Finally I came up with one of my bright ideas. "Kids," I said, "let's pray about it and lay a fleece before the Lord." They avidly agreed.

By saying "fleece," I was of course invoking the example of Gideon's fleece, from Judges 6:36–40. In that passage, Gideon asks God, as a sign of assurance, to soak a fleece with dew while the ground all around remains dry. And the Lord did just that. It shames me a little to say so, but I think I was about to make a deliberately outlandish request.

"Lord," I prayed, "the children feel that we should have a cat. I disagree, so we are coming to You for direction. Father, if we are to have a cat, I am asking You to have a kitty walk up our pathway straight to our door. Amen."

"And, Lord," added Ginger, "please make him black." Her addition didn't worry me. By now I was sure my prayer was sufficiently *un*answerable.

More than a month went by. No cat. I figured I was in the clear . . . until the day I walked across the street to visit with a friend. As I rang her doorbell—with my back turned to my own house—I heard hysterically gleeful cries behind me.

"Mom, Mom, Mom! Look, look, look!"

I turned to look back. There, wobbling up my pathway, was a tiny kitty. A *black* kitty no less. The Word of God says "faint not." I tried not to. The kids started jumping up and down. "Thank You, Jesus," they cried.

My friend opened her door just as the black kitty walked through *my* door. "I can't believe this," she laughed, having learned earlier of my ruse. "That's the Lord's Cat."

And so he was . . . and still is at age eleven. Named "Meow-buddy," he has never run away, never gotten stuck in trees, never clawed my upholstery, and is, most amazingly, agreeable to any and all kinds of cat food. I guess you could call our black cat golden.

The Miracle of Asking

JOSE CASSERES

I had paused briefly under the portico of the old church to button my overcoat against the biting December rain. Who could ever guess the extraordinary reason that had brought me fifty blocks uptown from my Wall Street office on a day like this? As I wrestled with the facts, I tried to convince myself that the whole thing made sense.

Over that weekend, twenty-five of us belonging to the Young Marrieds Fellowship of the Marble Collegiate Church had gone to a retreat center fifty miles away from New York City. It had been a time for fellowship, meditation and prayer.

Then on Saturday night, responding to the challenge of a young attorney, we'd agreed to a daring experiment. For six months, with no strings attached, no holding back, we would surrender to God the most compelling need in our lives. With lawyerlike precision, he outlined the terms of our agreement. We were unreservedly to put our most heartfelt need in God's hands, praying daily for one another as well as ourselves.

To seal our agreement, we wrote out this need on a slip of paper and placed it in a self-addressed envelope. "As you write this down," he said, "pray that this desire will lodge itself deeply in your subconscious mind." The church secretary would be asked to mail the envelopes back to us in six months. My job was to deliver those twenty-five envelopes to the church. I now faced my own secret doubts.

"How," I asked myself, "would our group of spiritual novices ever maintain the serious discipline of prayer and faith necessary for such an experiment?" For although the group had met every other Tuesday for several years, most of the experienced ones had moved away, and their places had been taken by others, eager for spiritual discovery, but beginners nonetheless.

Back in the office, I faced the mountain of detailed paper work that is my daily fare in the export-import business. Then, as that day spilled over to the next and the next and the weeks eased into months, all thought of the experiment slipped from my mind.

I was diverted, not only by the computer-paced life of the city with its endless demands for my time and attention, but I also became increasingly overwhelmed by worry and fear over my job. My boss and I seemed locked in a ceaseless conflict over company policy. Our verbal fist fights became a daily occurrence. What began as mere disagreement mushroomed into a full-scale war.

Finally one day the tension reached the boiling point. He exploded. I exploded. Furious, I walked out of the office and down the hall, searching frantically for momentary seclusion and a chance to cool off. In desperation I locked myself in an empty office. On my knees, I pleaded, "O God, give me an answer to this!"

Within minutes I felt under control. A strange inner calm encompassed me. I walked back down the hall to the boss's office to get my paycheck. And then I got the news. I was fired—as of that moment. Curiously there was still no panic, no fear, not even resentment. Instead, I felt relieved.

With calm precision—although I was keenly aware of what it meant to be out of a job in the middle of a recession—I cleaned out my desk and headed home. As if under someone else's direction, I found myself at the stationery store buying a typewriter. Once home, the realization dawned on me. *This is what I've always wanted—a chance to be self-employed. Today I start my own export-import business.*

I cleared my desk to make room for the new typewriter. And that's when I saw it. The dime-store envelope, self-addressed, lying face up on the top of the day's mail, the letter I had mailed to myself six months before. I ripped it open. There in my own handwriting was my earnest plea—"the courage to start my own business."

Was it coincidence or an answer to prayer? My mind telescoped to that Saturday night meeting. Could there possibly be any connection between today's events and that long-forgotten request we'd made to God? There was only one way to find out—to hear the reports of the others at next Tuesday night's meeting. Finally the appointed hour for the meeting arrived. Seated informally about the room were sixteen of the original twenty-five.

After a brief prayer, I opened the meeting, reciting, as calmly as possible, the circumstances that had led to my self-employment. I didn't have too much time to gauge the group's reaction before Gerry Mengel was talking.

His strawberry blond, freshly grown mustache moved as he blurted out his story. "I have to confess," he started, "like Jose, I forgot all about our prayer pact, but that's what makes my story even more amazing."

He began by reminding us that at the time of the retreat he'd been given just six months to find a new job. Prodded into action by some of the men in our group, he'd finally written a resume and set up appointments for interviews. Then just a few days before our meeting, his boss called him in with startling news. They'd found a spot for Gerry in their Philadelphia office. Believe it or not, the very day he got this news he'd gone home to find his own self-addressed envelope. It's message? "How can I get a job in Philadelphia, so I can be close to my family?"

Betsy Lehman, a tall, poised school nurse, was talking. Six months ago, her situation had seemed hopeless. Released at midyear in an "economy move," she had sought positions in a number of places without success. She had printed in large letters on her slip of paper just one word, "job." Recently she told us she had unexpectedly been offered a much more challenging position teaching nursing at a local college. At first she'd been scared, but like me, she was relishing this new opportunity.

Jim Wightman, a salesman, was the next to report. As far as I knew Jim had never uttered a prayer in his life. He was the newest member of the group and just seemed to sit quietly in each meeting absorbing it all. But now he came to life.

Like me, Jim had lost his job only to discover that it was a blessing in disguise. Not only had he been led to start a new career in mutual funds, which he was finding highly rewarding but the whole experience had also brought his family together. His wife was helping at home, doing a lot of his secretarial and telephone work. The kids were even hand-addressing circulars. Jim was exuberant.

Not all the answers to prayer involved jobs. One advertising man told how he and his wife had learned to communicate better. Others told of relationships that had straightened out.

Sally Jamieson, a grade school teacher, was the last to report. She had been our resident skeptic, always asking us to demonstrate the reality of our faith, demanding us to "prove it." Annoying as this had sometimes been, we all knew we needed it; Sally kept us honest.

In her clipped New England accent Sally told of her answer. "It happened," she said, "the very day I received my envelope."

The teachers of the school where Sally worked had had their monthly meeting that afternoon. Typically, these meetings were full of rancor. Nobody trusted anyone else, there were rigidly maintained factions, the principal was indecisive and little was accomplished. But on this magical day things had been different. People had listened to each other. Decisions which had been postponed for months were finally made. The principal had shown new courage and had taken a stand on some important issues. By the end of the meeting, everyone in the room was aware of a new sense of community, a new respect for each other as people. It all seemed like a miracle, she said.

When she got home and opened the day's mail, Sally was stunned. She read what she had asked for six months before: "Closer cooperation and teamwork among the teachers."

It was an incredible meeting—and an incredible report. What had happened really? We were spiritual neophytes, untrained in matters of faith, undisciplined in prayer. We had solemnly agreed on a prayer pact and some of us had done better than others. Yet despite our inconsistency, God had honored our prayer requests. Why?

None of us had a good answer. Yet in looking back we have learned a few things. In the first place, the long-ago Saturday night session, when we searched our hearts and offered our greatest need to God, was power-packed. We meant business and God knew it. And our prayers that night helped each of us to see our heart's desire clearly and fix it firmly in our subconscious minds. Even though our conscious minds were more aware of day-to-day problems, the prayer was continuing in the back of minds.

There is another explanation. When we go to God unreservedly with our deepest need and what we desire is in our best interest, He is eager to help us. The reason is simple; He loves us.

The House That Was All I Could Have Asked For—and the Funny Thing Is, I Did

ELLEN AKERS

In 1972 my husband began working on a new job in Winnemucca, Nevada. Returning to our home in California from a weekend house-hunting trip in that area, I felt terribly discouraged. No money to buy a house, nothing available to rent. I flopped into a chair in the dining room and gazed despondently out the window. *What now?* I thought.

My mind began to churn. Wasn't God supposed to help people in trouble? What did I really know about God anyway? I had taught children in Sunday school that God is love; that He cares. But was I really sure? Did He care about a home for my family and me? Did He *really* care? Now was the time to find out. I got down on my knees.

I poured out my frustrations and hopes that Monday morning in my dining room in California.

"O Father, after so many years of tiny houses, I would just love something bigger—at least a living room and four bedrooms. Our two boys could each have a bedroom and I could have a sewing room."

The more I thought about it, the more excited I became. My mind ran ahead of my words as I visualized the little things that would mean so much to me. "A big yard and lots of trees. It would have to be terribly cheap rent because we're so broke right now and I really don't care how old and beat-up it is—just an old barn would be fine!"

All week I had such a feeling of anticipation and excitement—

like a little girl with a big secret. I didn't know what would happen, but I could sure dream.

The following Monday morning I was sitting in the same old chair, and the thought occurred to me that quietly, inside myself, I could dedicate a part of this dream house to God. But what part? "Father," I began a little sheepishly, "if there were *five* bedrooms, we could use that extra one for a foster child or anyone who needed a home. But You know that my husband has never been much for having people in our home for long periods of time, so You'll have to work it out with him."

That afternoon the phone rang. It was my husband Ray calling from Winnemucca. We had talked about how nice it would be to have four bedrooms but he knew nothing about my five-bedroom prayer, let alone all the details.

He was quite excited and said, "Just listen to this. I was walking down the main street today and I saw a 'house for sale' sign in the window of Glenn's Camera Shop. I went in and asked about it. He said I probably wouldn't be interested because it was sort of an old barn. But I wanted to see it anyway, so we went up just to look. As soon as I saw it I knew you'd like it."

"And it has five bedrooms, right?" I quipped.

"Yes, it does," he answered quickly, then hurried on to tell me more of the details of his find. "The living room is thirty feet long and there's a big yard, lots of trees, a large garage, laundry porch, all those bedrooms. It's not in real good shape, but we can take care of that later."

I stood there trying to get things organized in my mind. Was this *the house?* No waiting, no trials?

"But we have no money," I said.

"Oh, that's all worked out," Ray rushed on. "Glenn is financing it for us at payments we can afford and my old truck will be the down payment. We can draw up the papers this afternoon and sign them in the morning—that is, if you don't mind buying the house without seeing it." Then he added cautiously, "Honey, you know the fellow I've been staying with here? Would it be okay with you if he came and stayed with us for a while? We do have that extra bedroom."

The next morning, one day after I'd said the five-bedroom prayer, the house was in our name.

A few weeks later I made a trip to Winnemucca to see the house. I pulled up in front of it and prepared to feast my eyes. It was just an old blue house with a lilac bush trying to leap over the fence, but it was beautiful to me. My heart went up in joy as I thanked God.

As we settled into our new house further blessings revealed themselves—a lot of them things that could only have meaning for me: a playhouse for the kids; producing fruit trees so that I could can; a wonderful nook in the kitchen; a cubbyhole in the entry hall that is just right for my potbellied stove.

When the extra bedroom was empty again, we arranged to keep three small foster children in our home. Tracy and Theresa were blond, blue-eyed, three-year-old twins. Veronica was their tiny sister.

God continues to work in our family now that we depend on Him. And I'm sure He has provided us this old blue house so we might do His work, too, sharing our love and our home with those He sends to us. For now I know He cares about His children, He really does, down to the last detail.

Prayer

MARGARET BAILEY

God, give me sympathy and sense,
    And help me keep my courage high.

God, give me calm and confidence,
    And please—a twinkle in my eye!

Part Two

Praying With and For Each Other

Introduction

I urge . . . that requests, prayers, intercessions and thanksgiving be made for everyone.

1 TIMOTHY 2:1, NIV

We don't have to use special words to pray—but we do need to ask for the right things. If we pray for God to change our spouses, or our families, He may not do it until we are willing to be changed ourselves.

Prayer not only can change the climate of a family relationship, but it is the cement that holds a family together and protects it. Prayer sustains families through times of suffering, pain and separation, and is the most important gift we can give our children.

When we pray for one another, whether in groups or individually, lives and communities are changed. People have found jobs, labor and management have worked together for the better, and individuals have been transformed and given direction because they were part of a prayer group or were prayed for by committed Christians. As one woman found out, "Prayer works. It works wonders."

5.

Prayer and the Family

When Father Prays

When father prays the house is still,
his voice is slow and deep.
We shut our eyes, the clock ticks loud;
so quiet we must keep.

Sometimes the prayer gets very long
and hard to understand,
and then I wiggle up quite close,
and let him hold my hand.

I can't remember all of it,
I'm little yet, you see;
but one thing I cannot forget,
my father prays for me.

AUTHOR UNKNOWN

The Comfort of Prayer

CHARLES R. HOLLIS

Mother and Dad's fiftieth wedding anniversary was marred by Dad's health—recently he had suffered a heart attack and we feared another. That night, upstairs in my room in their farmhouse, I worried about my folks.

Life had often been difficult for them. Of five sons and one daughter, two sons were lost in the war; a third returned to them a casualty. Their love helped him to recover.

"Why more sickness and trouble for them when they've spent their lives doing so much for others?" I asked myself now.

Suddenly I heard voices downstairs. It was late and the sounds—though soft—startled me. Perhaps Dad had had another attack.

I got out of bed and hurried down the stairs to see if I were needed.

Halfway down I stopped. The soft murmur was distinct now and I could hear the words:

"Thy kingdom come, Thy will be done . . ." Mother and Dad were repeating the Lord's Prayer.

Leaning over the bannister, I could see Dad sitting in his chair with Mother kneeling beside him, her hands lightly placed on top of his as if enveloping him in love. I couldn't see Mother's face but Dad looked peaceful and content as he said the words.

I stood still for a second or two and then turned quietly and went back to my room.

It was more than an act of faith—their prayer gave me understanding that replaced fears and questions. Later I was able to cope with illness and discouragement by the memory of that night.

Mother and Dad had not been troubled. They still had God's Presence to comfort and sustain them, just as they had had all their fifty years together.

Picnic Pick-Me-Up

PRISCILLA DAVIS

My husband, Gary, an electrician, had been laid off from his job. Less than a week later, things became even bleaker when he fell through a cattle guard and crushed his leg. He'd be hobbled for several months.

In time I found a job feeding and watering eight thousand chickens. As Gary recovered and didn't need his crutches anymore, he got a job spraying herbicides on farmers' fields. But even though we were both working and meeting our bills, Gary couldn't shake his depression. He brooded; supper became a silent time. I felt empty and went so far as wondering if I should have married him.

A month passed, and I constantly begged God to change Gary. I wondered, though, if God could reach my husband, a man who'd never had much patience for talk of faith. In any case, there seemed nothing I could do. And then one morning, as I knelt to dust the coffee table, I heard a still voice saying, *Pricilla, do you want this marriage to work? Well, then, get up. Go fix Gary a picnic lunch and find him in the field.*

I packed a large woven basket full of Gary's favorite foods. Our three-year-old son, Christopher, and I hopped into the car, then went bumping along the rough back roads. We spotted Gary and waved. Gary swung the tractor around, struggled to get off and then limped toward us, a big grin already spreading across his face.

Where would we picnic? "There's a little shaded churchyard down the road," Gary said. "Why don't we go there?"

We came to a country church, sitting atop a little knoll. We ate our lunch under a big ash tree. We talked and laughed as our small son climbed on the churchyard stones. After the meal we quietly peeked inside the church. It was musty smelling but peaceful—a peace that I watched take hold of Gary.

For the next month God showed me new ways of caring for my husband: a simple squeeze of the hand, helping in the fields so that Gary wouldn't have to get off the tractor to fill the spraying tanks.

Fall came. Gary was called back to his electrician's job, and it was there that a man shared the gospel with him. I'll never forget the evening Gary rushed home, dropped his lunch box on the counter, found my Bible and began to read.

He hasn't stopped since, and our family has undergone a deep change. All for the better. And where did the change begin? Not in Gary, as I had prayed. No, God in His wisdom answered my prayer by changing *me* first.

From now on I hope I'll know better. Whenever I want someone else to change, I'll stop and say, "Tell me, Lord, should the change really begin with me?" *Yes* will be the most likely answer.

The Coffeepot Experiment

CATHERINE MARSHALL

The scene is forever etched in my memory. It was a winter evening, 1959, soon after after my marriage (after ten years of widowhood) to Leonard LeSourd. The setting was our new home in Chappaqua, New York, a sprawling white house with red shutters. We were gathered around the dinner table for our first meal as a new family with Len's three children: Linda, age ten; Chester, six; Jeffrey, three. My son, Peter, nineteen, was away at Yale University.

I had lovingly prepared food I thought the children would enjoy—meat loaf, scalloped potatoes, broccoli, a green salad. Len's face was alive with happiness as he blessed the food.

But then as Chester's big brown eyes regarded the food on his plate, he grimaced, suddenly bolted from the table, fled upstairs and refused to return.

"Let him go, Catherine," Len said. Then, seeing the stricken look on my face, he explained ruefully, "I'm afraid my children are not used to much variety in food. Mostly I've just fed them hamburgers, hot dogs, or fried chicken from a take-out place."

Had Len and I but known, that disastrous scene was but a foretaste of what lay ahead. Linda's hostility toward her new stepmother was all too apparent. The two boys wanted to room together, yet were forever fighting like bear cubs. One night when they started scrapping again, Len summarily removed Jeff to another room. The little guy sobbed himself to sleep.

Later on that same night after Len and I, exhausted, had just fallen asleep, the shrill ringing of the telephone awoke us. It was

Peter. "Mom, I got picked up for speeding on the Merritt Parkway. I'm at the police station." We agreed to post bond for Peter's release.

Yet all these troubles were but surface symptoms, the tip of the iceberg of difficulties. Flooding in on us day after day were the problems of parents and relatives, together with the children's emotional trauma from six housekeepers in ten months. Even Peter was still suffering from the loss and shock he received as a nine-year-old when his father, Peter Marshall, died.

How do you put families broken by death or divorce back together again? How can a group of individuals of diverse backgrounds, life experiences and ages ever become a family at all? I knew I didn't have all the answers, but I also knew Someone who did.

So I began slipping out of the bedroom early while the children were still asleep for a quiet time of talking-things-over prayers, Bible reading and writing down thoughts in my *Journal*.

During those early morning times slowly there dawned the realization of something I had not wanted to face: Len was one of those men who felt that his wife was more "spiritual" than he, somehow had more Christian know-how. Len liked to point out that I was more articulate in prayer. Therefore, he was assuming that I would take charge of spiritual matters in our home while he would handle disciplining the children, finances, etc.

I already knew how many, many women there are who find it difficult to talk with their husbands about religion, much less pray with them. How could I make Len see that "spirituality" was as much his responsibility as mine? "Lord, what do I do about this one?" I hurled heavenward.

Somehow the answer was given me that nagging a male about this would not work. My directive was to go on morning by morning with the quiet time, but otherwise refuse to accept that spiritual responsibility for the home. The assurance was given me that God would work it out.

After a few more days, Len became curious about why I was getting up early. Persistently he questioned, "What are you *doing* each morning?"

"Seeking God's answers for my day. I know He has them, but I have to ask Him, then give Him the chance to feed back to me His guidance. You see, if I don't take time for this as the kickoff of the day, it gets crowded out."

"That would be good for me, too," was Len's reaction. "After all, we're in this together. Why not set the alarm for fifteen minutes earlier and pray together before we start the day?"

Thus an experiment began that was to change both our lives. The next day at a local hardware store I found an electric timer to plug into our small four-cup coffeepot. That night I prepared the coffee tray at bedtime and carried it to the bedroom. The following morning we were wakened by the pleasant aroma of coffee rather than an alarm clock going off.

We drank our coffee, and I started to read at a spot in Philippians. But Len wanted to get on with the prayer. "You start, Catherine," he said sleepily.

"But how are we going to pray about this problem of Linda's lack of motivation to study?" I asked. A discussion began. It got so intense that time ran out before we got to actual prayer.

Len agreed that we needed more time. Our wake-up hour went from 6:45 to 6:30 to 6:00. Discipline in the morning meant going to bed earlier. It became a matter of priorities. The morning time together soon changed from an experiment to a prayer-shared adventure.

By this time, Len, always methodical, had purchased himself a small five-by-seven, brown loose-leaf notebook. He began jotting down the prayer requests, listing them by date. When the answers came, those too were recorded, also by date, together with *how* God had chosen to fill that particular need. Rapidly, the notebook was becoming a real prayer log.

Not only that, as husband and wife, we had found a great way of communication. Bedtime, we already knew, was a dangerous time to present controversial matters to one another. When we were fatigued from the wear and pressures of the day, disagreements could erupt easily.

Yet when we tackled these same topics the next morning in an atmosphere of prayer, simply asking God for His wisdom about it, controversy dissolved and communication flowed easily.

Perhaps an actual page out of the brown notebook best tells the story . . .

Prayer Requests—
December 15, 1959

1. That we find household help so that Catherine can continue writing *Christy.*

2. That Peter will do more work and less playing around at Yale.
3. That Linda will be more motivated in her studies.
4. That Chester will stop fighting with his brother and accept his new home situation.
5. That we can find the way to get Jeff toilet-trained.

Morning by morning, the requests piled up and up . . . Linda's rebelliousness; a personnel problem at Len's office in New York; a friend with cancer; guidance as to which church to attend; a relative with a drinking problem; very close friends with difficulties with their children—and on and on.

We were learning more about prayer: that specific requests yield precise answers. So we did not simply ask for household help, we recorded a request for live-in help, a good cook, someone who loved children, who would be warm and comfortable to live with.

The day came when Len set down the answer to this in the brown notebook—middle-aged Lucy Arsenault. She was sent through Len's mother who had known her in Boston years before. Finding her enabled me to resume writing *Christy*.

The answer to Jeff's little problem came through the homely advice of the country general practitioner near the farm in Virginia. Irrepressible Jeff was simply too lazy to get up and go to the bathroom, too well-padded with too many diapers. Waterproof the bed, take all diapers off, let him wallow in wet misery. It worked—miraculously.

Now unless we had been recording both the request and the answer, with dates, we might have assumed these "coincidence" or just something that would have happened anyway. But with those written notations marking the answers to prayer, we found our gratitude to God mounting. The prayer log was a marvelous stimulus to faith.

Not that everything always worked out the way we wanted. We found that prayer is not handing God a want-list and then having beautiful answers float down on rosy clouds. God seemed especially interested in our learning patience and to trust *Him*, rather than man's manipulative devices for answers. Also, His timing is certainly not ours. Most answers came more slowly than we wished, and piecemeal. There continued to be some health problems. Two Marshall grandchildren died soon after birth. I worked for two years on a book I finally had to abandon. It took twelve years of anguish and many different kinds of prayer before Linda's life was turned around. But the turning point came with beautiful timing.

One of the best answers of those early days was Len's dawning realization that unless he became the spiritual head of our home, Chester and Jeffrey would grow up considering religion as something for the womenfolk. He had always considered his prayers too "bread and potatoes." But the boys liked that. So, as Len continued to say grace and lead the family prayer time, the boys began praying too—as if it were the natural thing to do.

Thus our husband-wife morning prayer time has set the tone and direction for twenty years of marriage.* That original coffee-timer (still operating although with many new parts) is one of our most cherished possessions. We know that neither one of us, or both of us, without God, have the wisdom to handle the problems which life hands us day by day. But as early morning prayer partners we have added assurance that "where two or three are gathered together" in His name, God is indeed with us. We know that communication between us, and between us and our children, has opened up. We can be sure that our morning prayers to God have mutual support and we know, from our prayer log, that those prayers are answered.

Why don't you go out and buy yourself a coffeepot and a timer? Try awakening to the pleasant aroma of coffee. Try approaching the problems of the day, partnered in prayer and with a fresh mind, and you may find—as Len and I have—a lifeline to cling to all day long.

How to Handle a Hard Day

RUTH WARD

Despite the hustle and bustle of a hectic world, our family has found a new way to make prayer part of our daily lives.

In our designated places at the dining table, each person prays for the person on his right every day for a week. The next week

---

*Written in 1979.

we switch to the person on our left and then the one directly across the table. Each shares particular needs of the day with the one praying for him. We also ask each family member to pick out his or her hardest day of the week. That day becomes the one when everyone prays especially for that person and his or her name is posted on the refrigerator as a reminder to all of us.

Kay, a senior in high school, chose Monday as her day because it's packed full with piano-practicing beginning at 5:30 A.M., then classes, homework and teaching piano students after dinner. Her day ends with youth choir rehearsals. She needs patience and concentration to get through it all.

On Tuesday, surprise solos are regularly on the agenda of the sixth-grade band, so Roger chose that day to let prayers bolster his courage.

Wednesday is Julia Beth's day because ninth-graders have all their major subjects on that day and she comes home weighted down with homework.

David, an eleventh grader, needs special understanding and patience on Thursdays when he makes his paper-route collections—whatever the weather.

Friday is Mother's day because after substitute-teaching all week, fulfilling the duties of a minister's wife and trying to keep straight a house that's becoming increasingly more cluttered, I need help to keep calm and organized.

Dad's day falls on Saturday when he needs special wisdom as he makes final sermon preparations and personal visits. Since there are only six members in our family, we award Daddy the extra day on Sunday because he needs special insight for his work at church that day.

One Friday, when the flu caused me to miss preparing breakfast and seeing the children off to school, I was gratified to find my name posted on the refrigerator as I was getting juice. If I fail to post a name, someone else usually does it.

But even the smoothest systems sometimes break down. At the end of one Wednesday, Julia Beth asked dejectedly, "Did anyone pray for me today? I didn't feel like anyone did."

Sure enough, her suspicions were confirmed—we all had failed her. We had forgotten to post her name and overlooked her in our special prayers.

Since then we have become more aware than ever of one another's needs and more concerned for each individual's problems. But most important, we are learning as a family the true power of prayer, believing in it now even more as it helps each one of us cope with whatever each new day brings.

Our Prayer Bulletin Board

MICHELLE C. HOLMES

The first thing I noticed when I entered the kitchen this morning was the sign on our bulletin board: one word in big, bold letters—PATIENCE. And I recalled that I'd put it there myself—just last night—because patience is something I need in my chaotic life right now.

Our family uses this kitchen bulletin board as a sort of central prayer-request board. In the past we've posted a photo of a starving child in Ethiopia (to remember to pray about the famine), a yellow ribbon (to remind us of the hostages), a picture of a special aunt (to think of her as she undergoes surgery).

Then, each night when we have grace before our evening meal, we can look at these mementoes and visualize who and what we are praying for.

"Pray one for another," the Bible tells us (James 5:16). In our busy lives, our family's "prayer pics" board helps us to do just that—and more.

Children of Pain

IKE KEAY

Today I work in a home for children, the only one of its kind in the country. It's a home for children whose parents are in prison. Many of these little ones have lived through cursings, beatings and broken bones. Some have even seen one parent murder the other. When they come to us, they don't know much about tenderness, about hugging. They do know about rejection and abuse. And guilt. And shame.

Here at Bethel Bible Village we give them love, warmth and a caring family atmosphere. We don't have dormitories, we have homes. But even when the children leave us, there's something else I can give them, something I discovered many years ago.

It seems so strange how all this has come about, that *I* should be the one responsible for these children. Though my life began differently, we ended up having a lot in common.

My younger brother and I were born in Scotland to the son of a successful dairyman and to a sensitive young woman whose parents had emigrated to America. Father was robust and hard-working; a good businessman and sportsman. My mother, Johanna Christina Keay, was gentle, delicate of health but strong of spirit, always ready to ease us through difficult times. I vaguely remember one of the most heartbreaking times for her. It was 1937, when I was five, and my brother, three.

We were waiting for Father to come home from work, when Mother took us gently into her arms to break the news: "Dears, your father has been in a hunting accident. . . . He'll never be coming home again. He's dead, and I think we must make a fresh start. So, I'm going to take you both to America to live with my parents, in New Jersey."

A few weeks later, we waved good-bye to Grandpa and Grandma, to the farm, and boarded a ship for America. Life there was rough. We lived in Newark, New Jersey. Mother's parents were not prosperous and were unprepared for the energies and antics of two young boys. Mother worked six days a week, while we stayed with our grandparents.

We had no money, but on Sundays, after church, Mother walked with us through a nearby cemetery, the most beautiful spot in our neighborhood. We played games and sang and daydreamed together. And while my brother and I snuggled in the curve of her arms, she read to us, often from the Bible.

Then, after four years in America, tragedy struck again: Mother developed tuberculosis, a disease that had already wiped out much of her family. "Please, *ple-e-ase*, let us stay with you, Mother!" I had begged over and over. "Please don't send us away!"

Three days later, her brother drove us to a children's home, and we cried all the way. Then we wept more bitterly, as we saw our mother ride away, leaving us with strangers. Little did we realize that she was going into a sanatorium and was not expected to live.

The home was on a farm of 212 acres overlooking a river and

a swamp. I saw the large dormitories—each housing twenty-one homeless kids—through a blur of tears.

I was taken to my dorm in a state of bewilderment and shock. *Oh, God, what is happening? Where is my mother?*

Finally that terrible first day ended, darkness came; mercifully, sleep ended my nightmare. But this brief escape came to an abrupt end as I heard a harsh voice barking, "Hey, kid! Get out of that bed! It's time to get up."

"What? . . . Who?" I asked drowsily.

"Yeah, *you*, Buck Teeth," yelled the gruff voice. "It's six-fifteen; that's when we get up here."

That was my introduction to the older guys. Because my buck teeth stuck out like a woodchuck's, I was called Woodchuck, or Beaver, or The Plow, for many of the years I lived at Glengary (not the school's real name).

The next day I was stopped by Mom Patterson, a small, stern woman, over sixty-five—so unlike my own mother—with a rasping voice: "Keay, did you see those boys smoking in the locker room?"

Mother had always taught us to be truthful, and so I naïvely admitted: "Yes, ma'am, they were smoking."

Later that evening the boys were waiting for me in the locker room. "So you're a squealer, huh? We're gonna teach you a lesson!" One of them twisted my arms behind my back, and the other guys began punching me. My knees buckled from fright and I cried out in pain. They only laughed and beat me all the more.

"We'll show you what happens to squealers, Buck Teeth," growled one.

"Oh, yes, I saw 'em smokin'," mimicked another in a high voice as he yanked my hair and pushed me against the wall.

When they had finished with me, they threw me on the floor. Once again I cried myself to sleep.

One morning I discovered I had wet my bed. The older boys found out and made fun of me. They made me take an ice-cold shower.

For days and weeks and months, it seemed *forever*, it was the same—the older boys bullying the younger ones.

I had never known such cruel treatment before, and I longed for Mother to come and rescue my brother and me.

"Stop that crying, you little sissy!" the boys would tell me.

Then they'd beat me some more, to make me tough, they said.

When I'd receive a letter from Mother, I'd feel loved again. She wrote to my brother and me faithfully, twice a week. Sometimes about the scenes from her window; sometimes about our father, whom we wanted to emulate because Mother described his attributes.

At Glengary, every child had chores before and after school and on Saturday mornings. Either carpentry and maintenance or gardening or husbandry. We raised our own food and did all the cleaning and repairs. It was hard; but it was good training. Then there were times to play, but I was afraid to enter in, because I was such a sissy.

One morning Pop Patterson told my brother and me, "You boys are going to the sanatorium to visit your mother." What elation we felt! It had been such a long time since we'd seen her. After a long drive, we were told at the sanatorium, "Sorry, boys, we can't let you go up to your mother's room; you have to be sixteen. Tuberculosis is highly infectious. You can stand beneath her window so she'll see you . . ."

We were not allowed to feel our mother's arms. Only to wave, and call up to her, and see her gazing down at us from her third-floor window. But her smile was full of love. And it was the most love I'd felt in a long while.

The years went by. I grew older and stronger, and I was not picked on as much. But I'll never forget the day when a gang of boys dragged me to the potato fields and demanded, "Okay, Plow, we want a bushel of potatoes, so start digging . . . and dig 'em with yer *teeth!*"

I struggled to get away, but they tied my hands behind me and held me down, pressing my face in the dirt. There I was, surrounded but alone, humiliated and called all sorts of rotten names, digging up potatoes with my huge buck teeth.

In the years that followed, we saw Mother only occasionally. The wonderful mother whom I dearly loved was slowly, tragically, becoming a stranger to me.

But her letters kept coming regularly, except when she had more surgery. Then we wouldn't hear from her for a month or so. Finally a letter would come: "My dear boys, my thoughts have been so much with you this day. . . . I send all my love. Remember, Jesus loves you, and I am praying for you. . . ."

Sometimes when Mother wrote, it was almost as if she knew

what was going on at Glengary. Like the time I decided to smoke on the sly because all the boys did it. You made your own cigarettes from corn silk rolled in toilet paper and lit them in a light socket with steel wool. Soon it became a regular thing with me because it got me in good with the big guys. But then one of Mother's letters arrived, saying, "Your father was such a clean man. You know, he never smoked or drank." So, at the age of twelve, I vowed never to smoke or drink.

"Hey, Keay, wanna go out back for a smoke?" a couple of the guys asked.

"Naw," I said, walking away.

"Hey, why not?" they asked.

"Oh, I dunno, I just don't want to."

As I grew, it became more and more obvious: I was becoming different. Instead of planning ways to run away from Glengary, I slowly began excelling as an athlete. My self-image gradually began to change. I began to do better in school. In fact, I ran for school offices and won. I applied for scholarships and got them. And I didn't beat up on the little kids; they came to me, for protection. I didn't understand it, or even think about it much. But I was different.

It was then time for graduation, time to take advantage of the scholarships I'd won and go to college. But I couldn't. Though I was president of my high school class, I left two months early to take a good job to support Mother, who was going to be released from the sanatorium in six months. It was up to me to make a home for her.

Tuberculosis had claimed many of Mother's ribs, most of both shoulder blades, half of both lungs. But Mother had held on to life, pain-racked and bed-ridden, so she could be with her two boys. After ten long years, we were together again, in Elizabeth, New Jersey, where I took a position with Standard Oil Company.

Morning after morning, as I passed Mother's room, I would see her slowly, painfully, kneeling by her bed. Her thin hands clasped, head bowed in prayer. And I knew that even as Mother's body had weakened over the years, her faith had grown deeper.

One morning, when she heard my step in the hall, she invited me in. Only then did I discover that during all the time we were apart Mother had been closer to me than I could have imagined. "Ike," she said, "God has been good. I see a fine man standing before me, a son to be proud of. God heard my prayers."

Mother told me how, in all the years that she could not be with us, she had prayed for us, constantly. "I asked the Lord to watch over you boys, to wrap you in His love. Ike, each day I pictured God's shield protecting you."

Then I knew. Mother's prayers had reached across the miles, protecting us, shaping us. A mother I had seldom seen had the greatest influence on my life.

Not long after this, I too met Jesus Christ on my "road to Damascus," as had the Apostle Paul. It was then that some of the missing puzzle pieces started to fit. God had allowed these experiences in my youth to prepare me for a new calling.

So I left Standard Oil and went back to Glengary as a houseparent to boys like myself—to show and tell them about God's love. Three years later I left to enter college to better equip myself for this new calling.

It was during this time that my mother went home to be with her King. God had been gracious and had given us six years together. Immediately following her funeral I learned the startling truth about my father. He had been discovered with a fourteen-year-old girl, an employee; and her father had called the police. They were on the way to arrest him when he took his shotgun and killed himself.

While I was still in college, I met my wife-to-be, Carolyn. After working a number of years in other children's homes, we moved to Bethel Bible Village in Chattanooga, where I was executive director; and we raised four children of our own.

Like the parents of the children at Bethel, my father had committed a crime. I can understand the disappointment and the shame these children feel. I know too how such a child longs for home and for affection. And I know the suffering that a child can endure in an institution. Surely that makes me more sensitive to these children of pain.

We do not have the children long at Bethel. By law they can stay with us approximately eighteen months. However, we do have some leeway, because one or both parents may be in prison for terms longer than that; but eventually each child must leave us.

And as each youngster returns to his home, frequently one of neglect and abuse, sad as I am, I know that I can go on helping and trusting. For I can go to my room and pray. I can ask God to wrap that child in His love, to give him or her the same kind of strong shield that protected my brother and me.

There is a supernatural power that we can draw upon. It flows through us in prayer. It is God's strength, the greatest force in all creation. I know, because I have experienced it.

Cornerstone

LYDIA O. JACKSON

The cornerstone of every home,
The most important part,
Is never laid upon the earth,
But in the mother's heart.

6.

Prayer With Others

The Day Thou Gavest Lord Is Ended

. . .

We thank Thee that Thy Church unsleeping
　While earth rolls onward into light,
Through all the world her watch is keeping,
　And rests not now by day or night.

As o'er each continent and island
　The dawn leads on another day
The voice of prayer is never silent
　Nor dies the strain of praise away.

JOHN ELLERTON
(1826–1893)

The Park Ridge, New Jersey, Experiment

ROBERT MILLER

I've always believed that God gives us cues for living, cues that we must be on the alert for, or we miss them. Over the years, those cues have directed my life in many major decisions: my faith, my choice of career, my marriage. In October 1980, God sent me another cue that I picked up on. It changed my life. And the lives of some friends of mine.

I remember it was a Thursday night; I had just returned to my room at the Los Angeles Hilton, exhausted from three intensive business meetings. As manager for a large communications corporation in New York, I had flown to the West Coast to coordinate a major equipment cutover for one of our customers. It was a complex job. I had always loved my work, but lately it seemed there was just one crisis after another.

While waiting to join my associates for dinner, I picked up a copy of *Guideposts* that the hotel provides for its guests. The story I opened to was about some men in Cincinnati who had business, unemployment or family problems but who found solutions after taking part in a "prayer experiment." I'm a committed Catholic layman—as a young man I had even felt called to be a priest—and I believe in prayer. So I found this story about ordinary laymen like me who used faith to solve practical problems intriguing. But then I went to dinner and forgot about it.

The next day on the plane, when I put my hand in my attaché case I came up with that copy of *Guideposts* again. Strange, I hadn't intended to take it with me; I must have picked it up inadvertently with my business papers.

"The Prayer Experiment." The bold red title leaped out at me. I had opened to that same article. Well, before I knew it, I'd read that story *again*. It was about a middle-aged architect, Herb Hilmer, whose business was failing. It seems he heard about a prayer group called The Pittsburgh Experiment, which has been ministering to businessmen since 1952. Hilmer and an unemployed friend prayed for each other's problems for thirty days. By the last day both men had been helped. That was the beginning of what today is The Cincinnati Experiment.

Could it be so simple? I wondered. *And why am I reading this article again?* At the end of the story there was an editorial note inviting readers to form their own Experiment groups. A nationwide organization was forming called The Guideposts National Experiment.

Back home in Park Ridge, New Jersey, the next morning, after sleeping late, I was romping on my bed with three of my kids when the phone rang. It was Rich DiLeo, an acquaintance, an enterprising young executive. At least he *had* been. "Bob, I've lost my job," he said. "I hate to bother you, but are there any openings at your office?"

I get a lot of calls from people with problems, because I'm involved in help-groups at our parish church. But this surprised me.

"Hey . . . I'll work cheap, Bob," Rich quipped.

"We don't have a thing, Rich, I'm sorry," I replied. "Say . . . try Jack Funesti." Jack, a mutual friend, was the vice-president of a perfume company.

"I tried him. Didn't you know? He's out of work, too."

"No . . . I didn't," I said. "But what about George Barker? I'll bet he'll . . ."

"Bob, where have you been?" Rich said, his voice now flat. "Barker lost his job six weeks ago."

That shook me. Three friends, all of them out of work! Then it hit me: *The story in* Guideposts *had mentioned unemployed men!* It sent goose bumps down my back.

Five minutes later I was in the kitchen, excitedly telling my wife June and one of our seven kids about Rich's call and the Guideposts story. "What an uncanny coincidence," June said.

"Honey, it was no coincidence," I said. "I'm sure the Lord was telling me something, but what?"

The next day at mass I prayed for an answer—one that wasn't long in coming. That afternoon while I was watching NFL football on TV, an idea popped into my head: *Why not write to The National Experiment?* The address was there in the Guideposts article. Then I wrote notes to those men who had lost their jobs, and to a few I had heard of in the meantime. I invited them over to my house on Thursday. I even wrote a note to Hugh Tuomey, a high school friend I hadn't seen in ten years. That was a foolish-seeming whim, but I mailed the letter anyway.

The whole thing was crazy. What was I getting myself into? *I* wasn't unemployed . . . I wasn't even sure what I'd do or say at that meeting.

The day before our get-together, a packet of literature arrived from The National Experiment—just in time!

On Thursday, my whole family got into the act. June made coffee and cookies; the kids hung around to help me greet the fellows at the door. Six men showed up—not bad for starters. Dennis, my son-in-law, had dropped by. He was having trouble with *his* job, so he stuck around, too.

Just before we began, I told my old classmate Hugh, "Maybe this isn't for you. I don't know what your situation is . . ."

"Bob," he replied, enthusiastically, "I've just changed jobs, and I think I've made a big mistake. I'm working with a bunch of *sharks*. How did you know I needed help?"

"I didn't," I replied.

As we settled down, there were jokes about résumés and being obsolete at forty, but once the meeting began, those men I had invited into my home were looking at me intently. They expected—*needed*—to hear me say something that would help them. I sent up a hurried prayer . . .

Beginning the meeting, I said, "This may be crazy, but we're here to try an experiment in prayer." Then I went over The National Experiment guidelines with them. We had to *accept* one another—"as we are, where we are." We had to be *honest* with one another, *sharing* our failures, our successes, our pain. We had to *trust* and *encourage* one another. There should be no criticism or attempts to give "advice."

We introduced ourselves. Each man told something about his situation. From the start we really tried to stay loose and let the Lord take over the meeting. And we felt His presence there, especially in the pauses, the silences. This in itself was unusual, because business executives are so "task oriented" that ordinarily we want to fill up every second with activity or talk.

"You know," Hugh said, after one of these pauses, "I like this sharing business, because when you're down and out you tend to focus on yourself and your own problems. Your fear isolates you, cuts you off. You begin to think you're the only guy in the whole world who's out of work. But it says here the Experiment requires that you pray about the *other* man, care about him. I think that's healthy."

Before the meeting concluded, each man was assigned a "prayer buddy"—a man he'd pray for, and who would in turn pray for him, daily, for thirty days. We agreed to meet each Thursday at my home at 8:00 P.M. to share results.

Things began to happen. Not suddenly, like magic, but gradually. As the weeks passed, men who had been bitter and withdrawn or whose boisterous laughter had masked anxiety, talked about their innermost fears and hopes. In the very act of sharing there was a kind of healing. We were experiencing the truth of St. Paul's words: ". . . to comfort those who are in any affliction, with the comfort with which we ourselves are comforted by God." (2 Corinthians 1:4, RSV).

And what were the results? Here are some of them:

· Chuck Garrison: Chuck, like me, had a job, but he had been unfairly passed over for promotion; he felt stagnant on his job and needed a challenge. We really prayed for Chuck. Over a period of weeks you could see the change in him, as he learned that he wasn't the only man who had ever been given a raw deal. Within five weeks of joining the Experiment he made a renewed commitment to the Lord. Then, quite suddenly, Chuck received not one but several good job offers. We were amazed at the almost immediate response to our prayers for Chuck.

· George Barker: George was one of the three unemployed executives who had started me on this whole Experiment. Within a few weeks of starting the Experiment, George received a job offer and relocated in Indiana. Again we were amazed at the quick results, and so was George. Yet, within a month, he called to say things weren't working out at all.

What had gone wrong? Nothing, actually. We were learning that God doesn't always move us in a straight line to our goal. He may want us to have learning experiences along the way. At any rate, we put George back on our prayer list. Within another month or so, he received a new job offer in Washington, D.C. He's been there over a year now, and he and his family are happy and settled in. But it took lots of prayer and patience.

· Jack Funesti: Jack was a vice-president who had been forced into early retirement. For years his hobby had been making picture frames. One night he confided to us: "Now that I've got time on my hands I've been wondering if I could do it profession-ally—you know, open a little frame shop." His eyes as he spoke were shining.

"Sounds like something you really want to do, Jack," I said. "Let's all be praying about it. Okay?"

Our prayers and support gave Jack the courage to take the plunge, to step out in faith to do the thing he had always dreamed of. Eventually he opened that little frame shop. Today, a year later, it's thriving. And so is Jack.

· John Doris: A bright guy who had lost one job because of a chronic back problem and was about to lose another. Like many troubled men, John's instinct was to crawl away and hide like a wounded animal. One night his wife called to say that John had been hospitalized for back surgery. "Bob, will you ask the men to pray for him, please . . . ?" I assured her we would.

Later, when the doctors were "prepping" John for surgery, they discovered that his back condition had "somehow" improved so dramatically that they canceled the operation! Today, John is well and has begun his own business. He is a core member of the Experiment, and one of our most vocal supporters. Not only did the Lord provide John with a job, but He restored his health, too.

I could go on and on with stories. Of course it would be misleading to imply that every man has had a perfect answer. God never promised riches or a long-term retirement plan, though He always supplies manna for the day. Some of our members have had to give up Cadillacs and caviar but all of us in this fellowship of like-minded men are learning humility, patience and the secret of letting God direct our lives.

It's been remarkable, this experiment in prayer. In the past twenty-two months twenty-one unemployed men have joined us. *Eighteen* of those men have found jobs! (We're currently busy on the other three!) So you see, it's worked for us. It can work anywhere—it can work in your town, with your friends, associates, neighbors—with *you*.

And what of me? I'm still working hard at my job, still being challenged. But I've found that reaching out to help others, and depending on the Lord for answers, has greatly lessened the stress and strain of my own work. That's what the Experiment is about, too—helping *employed* men cope with job pressures in the workplace.

I know that the feeling of pressure I had the night I first read about the Experiment in the hotel room has vanished. That was the night that God gave me a cue—I'm glad I didn't miss it.

Me, Lead a Prayer Group?

CLAIRE DONCH

In the winter of 1982–83 my husband Mike and I were in deep financial trouble. We had a lot of bills to pay, especially my own medical ones, and things had gotten so bad we were forced to accept food from my church and money from the local Christmas fund to buy our little girl Heidi a winter coat.

We weren't the only ones. We live in Erie, Pennsylvania, a town of a hundred twenty thousand. In spite of the corporate presence in Erie of General Electric, Hammermill Paper and Bucyrus-Erie, the unemployment rate was 18 percent! Mike worked for a cable TV company on commission; he received no regular salary, and though he was working more than fifty hours a week, his paychecks continually dwindled. So on weekends he worked as a saxophonist with a band, and I had a part-time job. But still, with the steady drain of a big medical bill and several other unexpected setbacks, we couldn't make it. Our problem was not *un*employment but *under*employment.

The day I returned from shopping for Heidi's coat, Mike came home for lunch with his co-worker Randy Weed. Randy enjoyed eating at our house; soup and sandwiches were a break from the macaroni-and-cheese he and his family were subsisting on. Mike had had a bad morning. Out of twenty-five calls, not one person had subscribed to the cable system. And while Mike was on his home-visiting rounds, one guy had actually thrown him off a porch.

I was heartsick as I made the sandwiches. As humiliating as it was accepting charity, at least we had been able to get Heidi's present. But it would be a slim Christmas at Randy's house. All at once I felt like crying—for us, for Randy's kids, for all the decent, hard-working families struggling in the recession that gripped the nation.

A few days after the shopping expedition, the November 1982 issue of *Guideposts* arrived. One of the articles in the new issue grabbed me. Titled "The Park Ridge, New Jersey, Experiment," it was about Robert Miller, a Christian businessman who started a prayer group with unemployed friends. I wondered if this sort of group could work for Mike, because the Experiment story told how good things began to happen for Bob Miller and his friends as they prayed together about their common problems. Most of them found jobs; all were strengthened and comforted.

When Mike got home that night I asked him to read the Miller story. He didn't want to at first. Mike, who's a church-going Catholic, believed that *Guideposts* was for—and about—Protestants. (I myself am Protestant, a member of Wesley United Methodist.) I persisted and Mike finally read Bob Miller's story.

Initially he wasn't impressed. But the next day he went back and read the story again. A nagging feeling told him he had missed something; it was that Bob Miller, too, was Roman Catholic. They had something in common. And Mike related to the problems of the men in the story. True, he had a job, but the financial stresses were the same.

I was surprised when Mike suggested that we write to the Guideposts National Experiment, the organization that gave Bob Miller's group its guidelines.

Soon we received a letter back, with suggestions for starting a prayer group. We found that the basic idea of the Experiment is that partners pray for thirty days, seeking answers to each other's problems. The guidelines suggested that newcomers start small by praying with a single partner. So Mike—who'd always been unwilling to pray aloud, even with me—asked Randy if he would pray with him. And I called up my minister's wife, Judy Schmidt, and asked her if she'd try the Experiment with me. Both agreed.

We began our prayer experiment in earnest. We knew, though, that we couldn't just pray and then sit, waiting for something to drop out of the blue. The cable TV job, for instance, was not going to improve; prayer helped Mike face that harsh fact. And so, though he had always hated job-hunting, he now attacked the want-ads with enthusiasm.

Thirty days went by and at that point Mike and Randy were so encouraged that they got some friends together and began a prayer group. If anybody had told me six months earlier that these rough-tough former cocktail-lounge musicians would be praying together, I would have laughed. But there they were, with bowed heads, talking to God about one another's hurts and needs.

A week after starting his prayer group, Mike was called in for an interview with a top national insurance company. The job was just what he had been hoping for.

While Mike waited for an offer, he was optimistic and full of faith. But I was more anxious and frightened than ever. Despite the fact that Judy and I were praying together, I was calling her two and three times a day, trying to cope with my feelings, because *I* was the one facing the bill collectors; *I* was the one wrestling with a tight budget, trying to feed our family on next to nothing, caring for Heidi and running our home.

I began to think: *We wives bear burdens with our men, and we encourage them. But who helps us bear our own burdens, who encourages us? Where do we get support?* Suddenly an all-too-obvious idea popped into my head: *Why not start a prayer group for wives?*

I asked Mike what he thought about my forming a group. "Sure," he replied. "You can do it, Claire." But then I hesitated, asking myself, *Am I really capable?* I've had a high-frequency hearing loss since birth, and I often rely on lip-reading. Because of this, when I become nervous, my speech tends to get garbled. My previously strong faith was wavering at this point, so how could I hope to lead a prayer group?

"Mike, suppose I make a mistake, forget what to say?"

"So what? Wing it." He wasn't letting me off the hook.

"I'm not a leader," I protested.

"Honey, we salesmen have a saying: 'You have nothing to lose and everything to gain, so pick up the phone and dial.' "

So that's what I did. I knew Judy would join the group. Who else? Linda Webber was a minister's daughter . . . she wouldn't think I was a religious fanatic.

Linda was supportive. Even though she had three part-time jobs and a young son, she found the time to give the group a try. With two positive responses, I got the courage to dial seven more numbers. One more person accepted.

I read and reread the National Experiment guidelines until I had memorized them. The first meeting of our women's prayer group was held at our home. There were four of us: three Protestants and a Catholic. I opened with a short—a very short—prayer, asking God to be with us. My voice had a wobble I hoped wasn't too noticeable. Then, silence. I took a deep breath.

"Judy and I have been praying for more than thirty days now," I began. "We feel a need to support each other. Now, with this group, we believe we all can help one another by talking and praying about what is bothering us in our lives. Please don't feel you have to contribute if it makes you uncomfortable. But I'll tell you what's happened in my life . . ."

Then, as simply as I could, I told my friends for the first time of the terrible pressures Mike and I had been facing. "But you know," I said, "Judy and I have kept a log. At the beginning of our Thirty-Day Experiment, it was filled with negative thoughts. Toward the end, most of our entries were positive. I feel better about things, and I think Judy does too.

"The concept in the National Experiment guidelines that encouraged me to create a women's group is this: *God will accept you at any level of faith or doubt.* If He can believe that self-conscious, sometimes tongue-tied Claire Donch can accomplish something, then I can believe it too! Think about it."

One of the other women spoke up. "Well, I'm not much good at praying aloud, but I need help. My husband is underemployed . . . just like Mike. And I'm having an awful time handling our three kids . . . You know, my oldest, Joey, is only three. I need more patience . . ." She stopped, suddenly embarrassed. Judy patted her hand in encouragement.

The other women began to open up about the things that were troubling them. Judy admitted she and her husband were having financial problems involving the sale of their home in New York City. Without the proceeds from a sale, they struggled to meet their current bills. She asked for prayer.

All at once I realized I had forgotten to be afraid! Instead, there was a beautiful feeling of caring in the room. And something even more wonderful—the presence of the Lord. He was there with us as we talked and prayed. The words of St. Paul came to me: "Bear ye one another's burdens, and so fulfil the law of Christ" (Galatians 6:2). And that "law" is simply to love one another. That was what we were doing. And that was why we felt Him there with us!

Before we closed with the Lord's Prayer, we agreed to pray for one another every day.

We decided to hold weekly meetings—and almost immediately we ran into problems with the husbands. Our meeting was scheduled at 8:00 P.M., just when one of the fellows was expecting his dinner. Another husband didn't fancy being a baby-sitter. But eventually we worked our problems out and have stuck to our schedule.

Since we began last spring, our women's prayer group has gained some new members; others have dropped out. We're a small group; we think the Lord wants it that way until we're a little more experienced.

All of us have financial and related problems. One new member works part time to help make ends meet. Her particular problem is that her husband has had to take a job in a distant city. Like many of us, she had taken on chores ordinarily done by her husband—having the car serviced and mowing the lawn. When her husband comes home weekends, she tries to avoid burdening him with problems, so she finds the support of the group indispensible. However, she has been concerned about managing her time better. She has asked the group to pray about it.

So it goes, week by week. When one set of problems is resolved, there are always new ones to share and pray over.

Why has our women's group thrived? I think it's because we're "other-directed." When you stop to think of it, married women with children to raise can become isolated and self-absorbed. We get caught up in our own family's problems; we're starved for interaction with other adults.

So the prayer group gets us out of the house and out of ourselves. We realize in a deep way that we are *not* alone in our problems. Not all of us can attend every meeting. Sometimes there are only two of us. But it doesn't matter. Jesus Himself said: "For where two or three are gathered together in my name, there am I in the midst of them" (Matthew 18:20).

And what about my husband and me? Well, before we joined the National Experiment Mike and I were, in a sense, leading separate spiritual lives. Now we're closer than ever. We have a new respect for each other's beliefs. We concentrate on our unity in Christ, not on the differences. And, oh yes, Mike *was* offered a job by the insurance company; he accepted and is now happier in his work.

Are you facing problems? Are you scared, unsure? You *can't* be more afraid than this scaredy-cat was! And if I could step out in faith, anyone can. Let me tell you—prayer works. It works wonders. But you may never know, if you don't try it.

Akron at 8:00 A.M.

WILLIAM DEERFIELD

It was snowing when I arrived in Akron, Ohio, on the Friday evening before Thanksgiving of 1987. The TV news predicted twelve inches before morning. Besides the annoyance of snow, I wasn't looking forward to my assignment; there was a good possibility I'd fail to get a story.

Before I left New York City my editor said, "Get me the answer to this: What's the purpose of prayer breakfasts? Are they just pleasant get-togethers where church people meet other church people and pray, or do they accomplish something else?"

Ron Glosser, president of the National City Bank of Akron, and chairman and one of the organizers of the breakfast I was to attend the next morning, met me at the airport. As we drove to dinner, he assured me the breakfast would go on as scheduled, at 8:00 A.M. Saturday.

Good luck, I couldn't help thinking, as the car crept along through a descending curtain of white. How many of those invited would leave a warm bed early on a snowy Saturday morning for a "worthy cause" event like this?

After dinner, as we trudged through the snow, Ron and his wife, Lily, insisted I cancel my hotel reservations and stay at their home. An hour later, sitting at the counter in Ron and Lily's cozy kitchen sipping coffee, I asked Ron how the prayer breakfast came about.

"It started," he replied, "when Pete Geiger, who's a writer for the Akron *Beacon Journal,* gave me a copy of Wayne Alderson's biography, *Stronger Than Steel,* by R. C. Sproul (San Francisco: Harper & Row, 1983). Alderson is the founder of Value of the Person Consultants, an organization that holds seminars nationwide to help bring about reconciliation between labor and management by using the Judeo-Christian ethic of respect and concern for each individual person. The seminars point out, for instance, that contract negotiations often break down because both management and the union become so rigid in defense of each's own viewpoint that they reach a bitter impasse.

"Reading Wayne's book," Ron continued, "I realized he had the same concerns I had in my attempt to help solve our economic and labor-management problems here in Akron, especially in the areas of contract negotiations and unemployment due to our declining industries here.

"At our church, when I suggested we have a labor-management prayer breakfast to get the 'Value of the Person' message out to the public, somebody objected that including *labor-management* in the title would be too 'divisive.' But our minister, Knute Larson, agreed with me that our focus would bring labor-management problems into a spiritual context. 'It's something that needs prayer,' he said.

" 'You mean, we'll actually *pray* at this thing?' somebody quipped.

" 'Yes,' Knute replied. 'We'll pray, have special music, speakers. The breakfast will be a symbol—a rallying point from which real change can begin.'

"So," Ron concluded, "after that, a lot of work had to be done to get a large representation of both labor and management to attend."

The next morning, the snow had stopped. Ron left early to help with arrangements. Later, Lily Glosser and I slipped and slid toward town in her car.

The breakfast was being held at the Tangier, the largest meeting hall in Akron. When we entered, the place was jammed in spite of the weather. I was thinking about what Ron had said about the economic situation in the Akron area. As if reading my thoughts, Lily said, "People are desperate for answers."

A few minutes later I was introduced to Tom Edminston, a Teamsters truck driver, from Local 24 in Akron. "Do you think a labor-management prayer breakfast like this is valuable, Tom?" I asked.

"Well," he said, eying my tape recorder, "if it's just for show, then we might as well stay home. As for the labor-management part," he continued with a rueful laugh, "boy . . . I'll tell ya . . . there needs to be a lot more prayer breakfasts between the two. Frankly, I'm antagonistic toward companies. Three years ago the firm I worked for pulled out of Akron." He also seemed bitter because he felt his union hadn't done enough to encourage his company to stay in Akron.

Just then Ron Glosser called the guests to order. Before Edminston disappeared into the crowd, he agreed to give me his reactions after the breakfast.

The program opened with an invocation by Rev. Ronald

Fowler, of Arlington (Ohio) Church of God, urging serious "contemplation of God's will" in the proceedings. Next, a gospel group called Divine Hope sang a hymn stressing the need for repentance. Then there were more prayers. Rev. Knute Larson, pastor of The Chapel, echoed the message of repentance. Referring to the hostility and bitterness that is sometimes present in the workplace, he asked God to forgive those who were guilty of this and to help all to learn to love one another. He concluded by challenging the guests to "pray for someone at work you don't like." Dr. William Muse, president of the University of Akron, offered "thoughts in the form of a prayer" on the need for better labor-management relations. A prayer of thanksgiving was given by Dr. Gordon Werkema, president of Malone College, who thanked God for "the opportunity and challenge to take seriously Your command to love our neighbors as ourselves."

After the prayers, there were "greetings" from local leaders of labor and management, including Ken Coss, international secretary-treasurer of the United Rubber Workers union, and County Executive John Morgan. Morgan told the guests that he had attended a Value of the Person seminar and he thought that "seeds have been planted."

Finally Wayne Alderson, the main speaker, was introduced. A tall, rangy man who looks like a cross between a coal miner and a cowboy, Alderson got right to the point: "In this country, I do not see 'labor-management relations.' I see a *lack* of labor-management relations."

He spoke of his father, a miner who fought all his life for the dignity of workers. Then he talked of his own forty-three years of struggle to bring about reconciliation in the workplace. "I stand before you," he boomed, "as someone who's had a *bellyful* of conflict in business and industry, of people saying that confrontation is the only way."

Alderson said he was convinced that such an attitude on the part of unions and management bordered on stupidity. He said that everyone—workers and managers alike—need to be respected and valued.

"When you leave here today," he concluded, "you have a choice: You can continue to do it in the human way of confrontation, of alienation. Or there's another choice—God's way: reconciliation, love, respect for others. The question you have to ask is not 'Can we bring about reconciliation?' A deeper question you have to ask yourself this morning is: 'Will I personally work toward reconciliation?' Think about it: *You* can make a difference where you are."

The applause was thunderous.

Then, after a brief time for discussion at our tables, the event closed with the five hundred guests standing and singing a rousing rendition of "How Great Thou Art." And their fervor made it not only a hymn but their own prayer of praise.

The comments after the breakfast were, without exception, enthusiastic and thoughtful. Dr. Werkema summed up the mood of many when he told me, "I had thirty-five guests here. I'm not sure all of them agree with the ideas expressed here, but they got something to think about—and to pray about."

Trying to get a viewpoint from labor, I looked around for Tom Edminston, the Teamsters driver I had talked to before the breakfast, but he apparently had already left the hall.

Something was still bothering me on my flight back to New York. People seemed to be challenged by the breakfast's speakers, but what about concrete results?

Thanksgiving and Christmas came and went. I made a stab at writing this piece, but it wasn't coming together. Then one morning I got a call from Ron Glosser, who had some exciting news. For the first time in memory, he said, two county unions had settled their contracts well before their December 31 deadline, and many people were giving the credit to the impact made by Wayne Alderson's seminars and the Labor-Management Prayer Breakfast.

So I placed a call to County Executive John Morgan. He confirmed what Glosser had told me. In the eight years he's been in office, Morgan said, both unions had prolonged strikes, and even when they didn't strike, contract negotiations always went down to the wire and beyond. But this time, he told me, Local 2696 of the American Federation of State, County and Municipal Employees had agreed to a contract two weeks before the deadline, and Local 1229 settled a few days later.

Then I called Sharon MacBride, president of Local 2696. She told me that the seminars and the prayer breakfast had "definitely helped" in their union contract negotiations.

"When John invited me to the prayer breakfast," she said, "quite frankly I didn't want to go. But Wayne Alderson cut through all the garbage. He doesn't try to placate either labor or management. He makes comments that neither side wants to hear. Yet they have to accept it, because what he's saying is true.

"After the breakfast," she continued, "I went up to John Morgan and actually thanked him for inviting me. I told him that with the decline of the rubber industry in Akron and all, the breakfast was a start toward doing something."

I still wanted to get the reaction to the breakfast from Teamster driver Tom Edminston. He represented the rank-and-file worker, the most vulnerable—and most skeptical—part of the labor-management equation.

I wasn't able to reach him until late the next evening. "Frankly, I didn't know what to expect that morning," he said, "but the prayer breakfast convinced me of one thing: to stop hating. Since then I've prayed for my ex-employer and the union. And things are a lot better for me now. Don't get me wrong. I still want justice done, but I'm not out for blood anymore."

I had my story now. Many people had been inspired—and changed—on that November morning; they had gone away from the breakfast determined to make a difference in their daily lives, on their jobs—plain ordinary workers, college presidents, union leaders, journalists, clergy, business managers.

Maybe, as my editor suspected, there are lots of different kinds of prayer breakfasts. But this one in Akron happened to focus on a real problem. As for his question, "What's the purpose of prayer breakfasts?" here in Akron I learned it was one more way to bring God where He should be—in this case right into the workplace.

The Four Days

RON ROSS

The baler *chunk-chunked* rhythmically behind me as I turned in the tractor seat to glance at our new neighbors walking past. Interesting-looking people, men with beads, women in long dresses.

Not that such things were unusual in Deer Island, Oregon, nowadays. Newcomers had begun moving here from Portland in the mid-70s. Nice enough folks, kind of kept to themselves. This latest group, for instance. When a bunch of them moved into the ramshackle apartment down the road, my wife went over with some homemade preserves. They seemed to appreciate it. Didn't ask her in, though. Didn't give their names.

Well, we sure didn't want to pry into anyone's business. Trouble was, some of the newcomers were doing things you couldn't help but notice. Two young couples who had come from Portland, for example, lived above and worked in the grocery store down at the crossroads next to an abandoned school and the church. Used to be you'd meet your neighbors there, stop and chat. Nowadays you couldn't hear a word over that booming rock music. You'd hand your money to the silent fellow behind the counter and get never a nod. His black hair went to his waist, and dark glasses hid his expression like a locked door.

Here in Oregon we don't like to think unkindly about people, but lately things had turned up missing from our toolsheds and barns. What concerned us most, though, was our young people. The grocery store had always been the place for kids to congregate; now it was even more so with the addition of a video-game arcade. Our kids were coming home with a whole new vocabulary.

"Daddy, what's a reefer?" "I think Tim acted sort of high in math class." The kids would laugh nervously as they unfolded bits of information around the security of the dining room table. Their mother and I found it difficult to talk even to one another about the changes taking place in our rural community.

The end of the row. I turned the tractor and, as so often before, tried to push the formless doubts from my mind. That very night down at church, however, they took on a shape and a name. I usually enjoyed these monthly deacons' meetings in the fireplace room. That night, though, Pastor Ray Anthony was frowning. "Friends," he said, "Deer Island has a drug problem."

He went on to report what was happening in the church's newly launched youth program. Attendance had been good, probably because there wasn't much else for teenagers to do. The program drew children from the "Portland people" too. From the beginning Ray had sensed something different about some of these youngsters. They joined in the discussion, but gave odd answers to some of his questions. Occasional hilarious laughter over nothing. A closer look confirmed his suspicions: dilated eyes, a telltale odor.

It was out in the open, the truth we'd all been aware of but hadn't wanted to confront. Now that Ray had broken the silence, each one of us had some bit of evidence to report. We were almost certain the two couples helping in the store were luring kids into drugs, first by giving, then by selling. For the most part it was not affecting the children of the congregation directly . . . not yet. And meanwhile, what about our relationship to the young drug users—boys and girls coming to youth meetings right here in this fireplace room? They were in need of help.

Over the next few weeks we learned that the problem was worse than we'd suspected. Many of the newcomers, it turned out, were longtime addicts. One night the state police set up a road barricade and arrested a man and a woman practically in front of our farmhouse. We learned later that both had served time in jail for drug peddling.

The following month eight of us attended a meeting called by Pastor Ray to decide on a course of action. But what action? What chance had we, a small rural congregation, against a plague that baffled even the experts? What could we do that we hadn't been doing all along—calling on these folks, trying to be neighborly, inviting them to various church functions.

"For all the response," one woman deacon said, "I might as well talk to the fence posts." We belonged to different worlds. In such a situation, what could we do?

"We can pray," Pastor Ray told us.

Pray? Well, sure, we'd been doing that too, individually, off and on. But since nobody had any better suggestion, the eight of us bowed our heads.

For a while there was some twisting about on the hard metal seats in that fireplace room. As the minutes dragged by, I grew impatient. Where was this getting us? We needed action! This was a case for the state troopers, or a federal narcotics agency.

Gradually, though, the fidgeting ceased; over the small fireplace room settled a potent silence. A living silence: the hush of a deep communion.

Thirty minutes passed. I'd never prayed silently this long before—or felt so connected to other people and to God. At the end of a full hour, a thought stood out in my mind that surely had not originated there.

A fast.

A fast? Like in the Bible? Like in Jehoshaphat's time? Yes, I remembered. Judah was being attacked by three powerful armies, and King Jehoshaphat proclaimed a fast for everyone. In the end, the attacking armies killed off one another, and Judah didn't even have to fight.

I looked up. Pastor Ray was standing. "It will be a four-day fast, then," he concluded for all the world as though there had been a discussion about it. I nodded wonderingly. How could this be? How could eight people reach a decision without a word being uttered?

Unless . . . unless in the silence God had spoken. And if God had spoken—then He was taking on our battle, as He'd taken on Jehoshaphat's! Starting now, Tuesday night, we agreed, the eight of us would embark on four days of concentrated prayer and fasting. This would be a brand-new experience for most of us, but there was a hopeful excitement buzzing through the room as we dismissed that evening. Our united request: that God would either bring these people to Himself, or move them out. As one man put it, "Move hearts or move bodies!"

The first day of the fast was pretty challenging for me, a part-time farmer and paper-mill worker who is fairly slim. I wondered if I would have the energy to finish the harvest. But I'd set my jaw and fix my mind on that prayer. I knew it had to be even harder for the women in our group, who were continuing to prepare heaps of fried chicken and biscuits for their large families.

The eight of us met nightly in the fireplace room for prayer and encouragement. And after that first day none of us felt hungry. What was more, our prayer-fueled hopefulness seemed to be mounting.

The four-day fast ended at midnight on Saturday. The next day, Sunday, we couldn't see any effect on the community; we reminded ourselves it was too soon to expect results. But neither was there any sign of change all that following week. In the grocery store the "Portland people" continued to look past us as though we didn't exist.

By the time my family and I took our places in church that second Sunday I was feeling pretty crestfallen—and a little ashamed of myself. What had got into me? I had been half expecting that some prayers and skipping a few meals could affect deep-seated patterns of addiction and life-style in people who were scarcely aware of our existence.

Beside me in the pew the kids were twisting around, staring toward the back of the church. I turned to look—and saw him, sitting just inside the door. Waist-length black hair; dark, emotion-absent eyes: the man from the grocery store. Quickly I faced front. "Don't stare!" I whispered.

At the close of the service, I hurried to the rear of the church.

But the man departed without a word of response to our greet-ings at the door. We "fasters" glanced anxiously at one another.

On the third Sunday, the man was back, this time with his wife and children. And they all went forward at the altar call! This family began bringing other families, reaching out to them as we had not known how to, "turning them on to Jesus," as they themselves put it. Many of those on drugs, we learned, had been miserable in that life-style. The excitement with which they passed on their newfound freedom to others was like something out of the Book of Acts. It wasn't unusual for a new convert to point across the now-crowded sanctuary: "Please pray for Jim and Polly over there. They need to know Jesus Christ." We more conventional churchgoers would cringe at these declarations, but offense was never taken—and often as not, Jim and Polly would indeed come to Christ! Users brought drug paraphernalia to Pastor Ray: "Please destroy these."

By now all eight of us were ashamed of asking God to "move hearts or move bodies." Watching how marvelously He could change hearts, we felt we'd been wrong to want Him to remove the others from our neighborhood. Moving bodies was no solu-tion; it simply changed the locale of the problem—perhaps to an area where no one was praying.

One bright Sunday morning, however, three months after that four-day fast, we were chatting in the church vestibule at the close of the service. The crowd of faces included one of the families from the store, smiling regulars now.

Suddenly Pastor Ray looked down the street and pointed. There, behind the grocery store, a truck was being loaded with furniture. The other couple, who'd persisted in their way of life, were moving away.

Without a word, our little group of eight filed into the fire-place room to give thanks to God for honoring our prayer, however deficient. We didn't know how He'd done it—whether through earthly means or heavenly ones. We only knew from the moment we "set ourselves to seek the Lord," we were like Je-hoshaphat: The battle was not ours, but God's.

Because it *is* a battle. Not, ultimately, against drug smugglers or organized crime or any other human agency. This is a spiritual assault and our most effective weapons are spiritual ones. I'm not a theologian, and I don't understand what happens when people start praying. But if prayer changed things here, maybe it can change things in other places.

Here in Deer Island, His orders to us were to fast. In another place He may have a different plan. But that He does have a strategy, a divine one shaped in invisible realms, we have never doubted since the night we grew quiet and asked.

Prevailing Prayer

RICHARD CHEVENIX TRENCH (1807–1886)

Lord, what a change within us one short hour
Spent in Thy presence would prevail to make!
What heavy burdens from our bosoms take!
What parched grounds refresh as with a shower!
We kneel, and all around us seems to lower;
We rise, and all, the distant and the near,
Stands forth in sunny outline, brave and clear;
We kneel, how weak! we rise, how full of power!
Why, therefore, should we do ourselves this wrong,
Or others—that we are not always strong—
That we are sometimes overborne with care—
That we should ever weak or heartless be,
Anxious or troubled—when with us is prayer,
And joy and strength and courage are with Thee?

7.

Praying For Others

Our Father . . .

You cannot say the Lord's Prayer
And even once say "I."
You cannot say the Lord's Prayer
And even once say "My."
Nor can you pray the Lord's Prayer
And not pray for one another,
For when you ask for daily bread,
You must include your brother,
For others are included in each and every plea;
From beginning to the end of it,
It does not once say "Me."

AUTHOR UNKNOWN

How to Feel Useful

CORA VIRGINIA PERRY

Last year I was hospitalized with a severe case of pneumonia. Since I was sixty-five and lived alone, I was transferred to a nursing home for the recuperation period. I was very weak and needed help with everything, even to turn over or sit up in bed. It was very discouraging.

One day, feeling utterly helpless, I complained to the nurse. "Why do I keep on living? What good am I? I'm just a nuisance. I can't do anything for anyone."

"Oh, I don't know about that, Miss Perry," she answered with a smile. "I think there is something you can do. You can pray for others."

What good medicine that was! There, flat on my back, I began to pray for my fellow patients, for the doctors and nurses, for world leaders, for anyone who came to mind. And as I did, I found I was moping less, and focusing more on the world outside. Without knowing it, I was getting out of myself, out into the world—if only in spirit. And eventually I was there physically too!

Today I'm living at home, and I'm able to take care of myself, but I'm still following that excellent prescription for feeling useful!

What Praying for Others Can Do for You

NORMAN VINCENT PEALE

Not long ago I had a vivid reminder of the power that can be generated when we pray—really pray—for others.

I happened to wake up at 3:00 A.M. on a Sunday morning. I had gone to bed early as I always do on a Saturday night when I have to preach the next day, but here I was, all of a sudden, wide awake. I tried every known device to go back to sleep. I counted sheep, I said the 23rd Psalm half a dozen times. But still I could not go back to sleep. Finally I got up at four o'clock, went into my library, and picked up one book and magazine after another. Nothing held my interest.

Some years ago in Switzerland, I purchased a large and beautiful eagle carved from a single block of wood, and brought it back to my library. Made by one of the old-time Swiss wood-carvers, it is really a work of art. The eagle has his wings spread and is taking off from some high eminence. I sat looking at the eagle, remembering when I bought it and the old man who made it, and then, naturally, I began to say aloud a passage of Scripture: "... they shall mount up with wings as eagles; they shall run, and not be weary; and they shall walk, and not faint" (Isaiah 40:31).

This in turn led to a thought about a friend, a pastor who says that occasionally, when he needs spiritual help, he goes into the church and walks the aisles. He places his hand on the pew where a certain person sits each Sunday and prays for that person by name. And he repeats the process at various pews in the empty church. The pastor says that this procedure always brings great blessing to him as well as to the persons he prays for. So, motivated by my friend's example, there alone in the early morning, I started to visualize everyone I should pray for.

The first person was my wife Ruth. Then I prayed for our three children and their spouses, then for our eight grandchildren. I prayed for all the relatives I could call to mind. Then my mind went to the church, and I prayed for the other ministers. I prayed for all the secretaries. Then one by one I prayed for all the elders and all the deacons. Finally I began to visualize the congregation at the church and prayed for everyone I could think of by name. Then I prayed for the doormen in our apartment house and for all the people with whom I am associated in any way.

Actually, I must have prayed for five hundred people by name. By this time it was 6:00 A.M. All of a sudden I felt better than I had felt in a long time. I was full of energy, and boundless enthusiasm surged within me. I wouldn't have gone back to sleep for anything. I was ravenously hungry and went and awakened my wife.

"Get up! It's six A.M.," I said. "I'm hungry, and let us have no piddling breakfast. I want bacon and eggs, the whole works!" And I ate a man-sized breakfast.

I went to the church and delivered a sermon and shook hands with hundreds of people. Then I went to a luncheon and gave a talk, and on to an afternoon engagement, and at eleven o'clock that night I was still going strong. I was not even tired! Such an excess of energy was mine as to astound me, and with it came a tremendous new feeling of love for life.

Now, I'm not psychologist enough to explain exactly what happened. I guess I got outside myself. Consciously, even subconsciously, I completely forgot myself in loving all those other people and praying for them and taking their burdens on myself. But this didn't add any weight, either. It added wings! And it left me happy and joyous, revitalized, reborn. Actually, I rose up "with wings as eagles."

So now, whenever I feel enervated or depressed, I repeat that prayer process. And I offer this experience as a suggestion of how you, too, may not only help others by prayer but also find marvelous new life for yourself.

The Navy Yard Secret

ANN ROOT

Some years ago my brother Burton held a job as a carpenter at the Philadelphia Navy Yard. His boss there liked his work, but one thing bothered Burton. The men swore all the time and, on the lunch hour, drank and made fun of Burton who, because of his Quaker beliefs, did not join in.

During the silent meditation period at Quaker meeting on Sunday, he asked God for guidance. We Quakers are taught to rely on Jesus' promise that "where two or three are gathered together in my name, there am I in the midst of them" (Matthew 18:20). And so we shut our eyes, relax, and listen; but first we usually say, "Father, I thank Thee that Thou hearest me always," and then we ask for what we need, just as we would ask another person. Burton told me later that he had asked God what to do about this problem at work—the drinking and the swearing— and these words immediately came to him: "God bless you and wake you up."

He took this to be the answer to his prayer; and so, to the first man that swore, Burton silently said, "God bless you and wake you up." Almost instantly the man stopped swearing. Later, as Burton repeated these words when other men swore or drank, they immediately stopped. Burton did not tell the men or the boss of his prayer, not even when he was transferred to another section and the boss told him how pleased he was, how the men liked Burton and what a good influence he had been. The secret was between Burton and God.

Knowing how this prayer worked for Burton, I have for years used it daily myself. I say it silently to everyone I meet. Although I never know how it affects anyone else's life, I know it helps me.

Instead of being critical or finding fault with people, holding them up to God for a moment in silence with a *God bless you and wake you up* keeps both the pray-er and the one prayed for in God's presence.

A Mighty Fortress

ROBERT J. "MUTT" OSBORNE

When I was an aerial gunner on a B-17 bomber flying out of England in 1943, we seldom came back from a raid over Germany or Occupied Europe without extensive damage to our Flying Fortress caused by German fighters or antiaircraft fire. That deadly hail of machine-gun bullets and shrapnel caused numerous casualties among crew members too. I remember we talked a lot about defensive armor, and wished we had some. Later on flak jackets were issued and did save some lives. But the most effective shield that ever surrounded me had nothing to do with armor-plated seats or bulletproof jackets. It was manufactured a long way from those furious combats in the sky. But without it I wouldn't be here today.

Let me tell you a little about myself. I was born in the low country of South Carolina, grew up on the hill of Puddin Swamp in the Turbeville community. Our family had a two-horse farm (took two mules to work it), but we lost it in the Great Depression when just about everybody went broke. My daddy had to fall back on sharecropping, and things were awfully tight. Nobody had any money; everything was barter, and there wasn't much to barter. We boys had to fish and hunt to keep eating. I remember being given the old shotgun and one shell—all we could afford—and told to come back with one squirrel or else face big trouble. When we went rabbit hunting we didn't take a gun at all, just a pocketful of those heavy square nuts that hold a wheel on the axle of a wagon. We threw those, and we got so we didn't miss very often.

My daddy wasn't much for religion, but my mother was. Everyone called her Miss Martha, and she used to say she was going to teach us young 'uns right from wrong if she had to beat it in with a stick. We went barefoot all week, and often shirtless too, but Miss Martha would round up all the neighborhood kids on Sunday and see that we wore shoes and went to Sunday school in the old Methodist church down at Turbeville. When the war came, she got all the church mothers who had boys in the service to meet every day and pray for our safety.

Because I weighed only about one hundred thirty pounds, my nickname was Mutt, after the smaller character in the famous comic strip *Mutt and Jeff*. When I graduated from aerial gunnery school, my size made me a natural candidate for ball-turret gunner. The ball turret, on the underside of a Fortress, was so small that the gunner couldn't even wear a parachute. You were down there with two .50-caliber machine guns and nothing else.

Some air crews were lucky. I can't say that ours was. On our very first mission we were shot up so badly that we crash-landed on the English coast. That was the end of our Fortress named *Little Chuck*. We got another named *The Last Chance*, and it almost was. On one mission, after we were hit hard, the bombardier and navigator decided to bail out. The bombardier pulled his ripcord too soon. The billowing silk streamed through the escape hatch and then pinned him against the opening so he couldn't move. He was just about being flogged to death. The wildly flapping chute came and tangled itself around my guns; I couldn't see or do anything. I had to go up into the plane, cut the bombardier out of his harness and pull him back aboard. I got a nasty slash across my hand from my own knife, but finally somehow we got back to England.

Early in November we were ordered to bomb Gelsenkirchen, a German industrial center in the Ruhr. It was my twentieth mission and it would be tough. I wasn't flying with my regular crew; I was a substitute gunner on another airplane.

We made it to the target and dropped our bombs, but then it seemed to me that the German fighters—Me 109s and Fw 190s— came in like a swarm of bees. I could feel our plane shudder from multiple hits, and when I swung my turret around to look at the engines, I saw that two of them were out. That meant we would be losing altitude and dropping behind the formation, a sitting duck for more fighter attacks.

I didn't hear any order to bail out (actually our communications system was destroyed), but looking down I saw parachutes begin to blossom under our plane. I counted eight of them. There were ten of us in the crew. German fighters were still coming in, but I figured if everyone was leaving I had better leave too. So I crawled up into the body of the Fortress and clipped on my chute, which I always kept right beside the turret.

The bomb-bay doors were still open, and I was about to jump when I happened to look ahead and saw the pilot slumped over in the space between his seat and the copilot's. It seemed to me that he moved a little bit, which meant he wasn't dead. For a moment I hesitated, torn between the desire to jump and save myself, and reluctance to leave a wounded man to what would be certain death. I guess my mother's lessons about right and wrong had been hammered in more firmly than I knew. I was frightened almost out of my senses, but I found myself walking along the catwalk above the bomb bay until I came to the pilot. He had been hit in the head either by flak or by machine-gun bullets and was barely conscious. The copilot had left the plane on automatic pilot; we were still flying on only two engines.

I knelt beside the wounded pilot, scared stiff and wondering what to do. I looked through the windshield to see if the formation was leaving us (it was), and as I did I saw something totally incredible. Reflected in the glass was a picture—a vivid picture—of a group of women gathered around a large dining-room table, praying. I knew who they were, because in almost every letter my mother told me she and her friends were praying. Even stranger, standing behind those women were their sons in uniform. I knew them too, and I also knew that some of them were dead, killed in action.

As I stared in amazement, the picture faded, but I heard—or seemed to hear—a commanding voice that spoke three words: "Take it back!" I knew it could not be the pilot, who was mumbling incoherently. I knew too that I was being ordered to take charge of our crippled airplane and fly it back to Britain.

But how could I? On practice missions I sometimes had been allowed to sit in the copilot's seat and "fly" the aircraft. But this "stick time" was insignificant. I had never attempted to land or

take off in a four-engined bomber, much less one with two engines out. But the voice came again, clear and authoritative:
"Take it back."

Now I seemed to be aware of a figure standing behind me. I
thought for a moment the tail gunner had left his position and
come forward. But that was impossible because I had seen eight
chutes. There could only be two of us left in the plane: the pilot
and me. But again the voice spoke, and this time it gave me the
compass heading for England. I think it was 322 degrees.

My reaction to all this, to the picture of the praying women,
to the resonant voice, to the inexplicable presence of a third man,
was a kind of total acceptance. My rational mind couldn't believe
any of it, but I accepted it. I felt as if a strong, wise commander
was giving me orders. It was my job to obey them, and I felt the
terrible sense of panic and helplessness begin to subside.

I crawled into the copilot's seat, took the Fortress off automatic pilot, and swung it around to the heading I had been given.
I still felt the presence of the third man behind me, but I didn't
look around. The formation had gone ahead without us. Off to
the left at about eleven o'clock I saw a squadron of German
fighters queuing up to let us have it. We were helpless and they
knew it.

Then suddenly, right ahead of us, was a towering cumulus
cloud. By rights that cloud wasn't supposed to be there; it wasn't
on our weather charts. But there it was, and we ducked into it
like a hunted deer. Visibility dropped to zero. No fighters could
find us in such cover. We flew along steadily, our two good
engines pulling us, and when we finally came out of the clouds at
about ten thousand feet, we were over the North Sea, and the
coastline of England lay ahead of us. A tremendous sense of relief
surged through me, and I glanced once over my shoulder. Was
that figure still standing behind me?

No one was there.

But we still weren't home. When we crossed the coast I began
looking for a place to try to land. I had no idea how to find our
own base, the 381st Bomb Group, but finally I saw a runway with
some transports on it. When I tried to talk to the tower, I didn't
know the proper call signs to identify myself, and they kept
telling me not to land. The Germans had been known to load a
captured Fortress with explosives and send it over England with
very little gas, hoping that when it came down it would blow up
something. The radio operators in the tower were women, and

I couldn't understand their British accents, just one emphatic word, "No! No! No!" I guess they couldn't comprehend my Carolina country talk very well either, but I hoped they would figure it was something no German pilot could possibly imitate. In any case, I had to land, because I was running out of fuel; red lights were showing on all the gauges. I told the tower I would circle once and then I was coming in. I asked them to have the crash wagon and the ambulances ready. Then I swung my big crippled bird in a wide circle and headed for the runway.

I was flying on only two engines, and the bomb-bay doors were creating a lot of drag, so I was moving at only eighty or ninety miles per hour. I didn't put the wheels down because I wasn't sure how to do it, and anyway I figured it might be safer with the wheels up. So I just eased her in, holding the nose up and letting the tail kind of sag. When I cut the power, the tail hit first, and then we skidded along on the belly of the plane, smooth as glass, almost to the end of the runway, where we just slewed around and stopped.

I got out of my window and went around and pulled the pilot out of his window. I put him on my shoulders and walked to the edge of the wing and jumped off; it wasn't very far to the ground. I was a little afraid of fire, but I knew we had almost no gas left, so I wasn't too worried. I dragged the pilot about fifty feet and fell down beside him just as an ambulance came screeching up. They wanted to put me on a stretcher, but I told them to take the pilot first. "He's wounded," I said. "I'm not." By now they were spraying the airplane with foam for fire prevention. Someone said to me, "Are there any more men on board?" I said, "I don't think you'll find any." Then a wave of blackness descended and I passed out.

When I woke up in the hospital, they fed me some broth and said I was suffering from total exhaustion. I couldn't quarrel with that. The pilot was badly hurt; he lingered a few days and then died. Before he died he signed a letter to our base commander recommending me for a Congressional Medal of Honor. They didn't give me that, but they did award me a Silver Star. And a long leave in London.

When I tried to tell our intelligence officers about the third man who had been on the plane, they smiled indulgently and said something about "understandable hallucinations."

I can understand their doubts, but I have no doubts of my own. I know it was our Lord Jesus Christ who came to me when

I was in terrible danger and told me what to do and helped me do it. I believe too that prayer put an invisible shield around me that day over the flaming skies over Nazi Germany. It can guard you too, if someone will just pray for you as fervently as that little group of women prayed for me. So many years ago. In a quiet rural community. On the hill of Puddin Swamp.

I Am Living, Breathing Proof

SANDRA SIMPSON LESOURD

In the living room of a cozy ranch house nestled next to the rimrock cliffs that border Billings, Montana, a group of women sat with clasped hands and bowed heads. "Dear Lord," Marlene said. "We're here to pray for Sandy. She's in deep trouble. She doesn't know we are praying for her, but Lord, we ask humbly that You be with her and strengthen her."

At that same moment, in the summer of 1978, I sat in Warm Springs, Montana, staring through the grime-streaked windows of the State Hospital for Mental Disorders. My weight was over two hundred pounds, my skin was gray and my hair greasy—a sad situation for someone who in 1956 had represented her home state of Vermont at the Miss America Pageant in Atlantic City.

How had I got myself into such a miserable condition? There's a lot of scientific jargon to describe compulsive personalities like mine. My motto since my teen years had been: Anything worth doing is worth *over*doing. I would tell people, "When my motor is running, I can't seem to shut it off."

And eventually my compulsive *over*doing resulted in debilitating addictions to everything from alcohol, prescription drugs and nicotine, to overeating and out-of-control shopping sprees.

"It's time to start," said Marlene. They were meeting again as they did every Thursday morning, these ten or twelve women from the First United Methodist Church in Billings. After opening with songs of praise, there were prayers of thanksgiving—and then progress reports about the people they'd been praying for. The meetings generally lasted about two hours, each woman bringing a notebook to record the prayers

they'd be making throughout the week. Special prayer attention was focused on the group's "Ten-Most-Wanted List," a list they had compiled, containing desperate cases of people most in need of the Lord: a teenager on drugs, a mother with Alzheimer's, a husband in the last stages of cancer, and a recent "most wanted" addition— Sandy.

So many people had tried unsuccessfully to help me: my family, friends, counselors and psychiatrists, including those at a treatment center where I'd spent a month. I put my head in my hands. It seemed hopeless. Could I ever go home? Would I ever be whole again?

Since the group believed in the power released by affirming the best in the person being prayed for, over and over they inserted Sandy's name into Scripture verses: "Strength and dignity are [Sandy's] clothing. . . . [Sandy] opens her mouth with wisdom, and the teaching of kindness is on her tongue. . . . Her children rise up and call her blessed" (Proverbs 31:25, 26, 28, RSV).

And then the women asked God "to transform Sandy, send Your emissaries across her path to witness to her, to free her from bondage."

I *was* in bondage—to a suicidal depression and spiritual darkness. Every time I closed my eyes, an inky black curtain fell across my conscious mind, and I was unable to summon any positive or pleasing visual images. It was terrifying to be lying in bed with my eyes closed and see nothing but forbidding night— or worse, evil, mocking faces.

One day a young woman named Karen entered the hospital and was assigned to a room adjacent to mine. Her fiancé, it was reported, had been killed in an accident. Karen was inconsolable. Over and over she kept crying out, "Help me, Jesus! Help me, Jesus!"

Karen's constant yelling was aggravating. And the worst thing was, she attached herself to me. I tried to avoid Karen, but she followed me, her dark brown eyes pleading for me to help her.

Then, on a sultry July night, I was tossing restlessly in my hospital bed, when I sensed a presence. I sat up. Karen was standing in the doorway, her white robe startlingly bright in the moonlight.

She approached my bed, crying softly. "Oh, Sandy, does Jesus love me? Does Jesus really love me?" I could tell from her pleading voice that this was the only thing in the world that mattered to her.

What to do? What to say? I longed to comfort this weeping young woman but felt incapable of reassuring anybody of anything. Yet I had to do something. Taking Karen in my arms, I stroked her damp hair. It had been a long time since I'd held anyone or offered comfort—I'd always been the one *demanding* it.

I cleared my throat awkwardly. "Yes, Karen," I said. "Jesus—"

I stopped in astonishment. My heart was beating furiously, I felt warm and cold at the same time. What was I saying to this young woman? Why were these words having such power over her—and over *me?* "Karen," I said. "Jesus loves you. He *really* does."

Her sobbing stopped in an instant. She wiped her eyes with the back of her hand, thanked me in a voice of childlike gratitude, and slipped out of my room and back to hers.

I lay back down, puzzled at the strange lightness, almost giddiness, that I was feeling. The room seemed filled with a fragrant coolness.

"[Sandy] opens her mouth with wisdom, and the teaching of kindness is on her tongue. . . . Her children rise up and call her blessed."
Thursday morning. The intercessors were meeting. "Dear Lord," Naomi said, leading the others in prayer, " 'God did not give [Sandy] a spirit of timidity but a spirit of power and love and self-control' " (2 Timothy 1:7, RSV). "And with his stripes [Sandy is] healed" (Isaiah 53:5, RSV).

A few days after Karen's nighttime visit to my room, she left the hospital just as suddenly as she had arrived. I puzzled about what had happened between us; for the first time in my long illness—and almost against my will—I seemed to have helped another person.

Was there something different happening to me? A glimmer of joy here, a flicker of wonder there? I'd been noticing the birds outside my window, a rose in a vase in the patients' lounge, the picture of a child in the recreation area.

I stared out the window into a small grassy courtyard. The morning sun had appeared over the building annex, casting shadows from a slatted roof overhang into my room. Across my skirt and onto the floor fell a pattern of stripes. Out of nowhere, words came into my mind: *And with his stripes we are healed.*

They sounded scriptural, but what did I know about the Bible? Could I have heard these words as a child in Sunday school? Strange, yet the words were strongly, deeply reassuring. Was it possible that I could get better after all?

Marge, Loretta, Eva, Dottie, Betty, Bess—the prayer witnesses were faithful to their tasks. Many of them prayed not only on Thursdays but on every day of the week too, sometimes aloud during morning and evening devotions, sometimes silently while waiting in line at checkout counters or sitting in traffic. Again and again their prayers went out: "[Sandy] can do all things in him who strengthens [her]" (Philippians 4:13, RSV).

To everyone's surprise, including my own, I was making such good progress that for the first time, the hospital staff felt I might make it on my own. A visit home was in order.

The first morning back in Billings in my own bed, I awoke terrified. How could I make up to my family for all my irresponsible behavior over the past fifteen years? Feelings of guilt and fear overwhelmed me. *Sleep in,* came the tempting voice inside my head. *Stay right here in bed.* That was the way I had handled things in the past.

But a new voice inside me spoke. *Get up and get going. Now!*

The old ways were entrenched, though, resistant to something new. I was afraid. No, I'd stay in bed today and start my new life tomorrow.

Get up. Do it now! The voice wouldn't stop—and I actually started to think I might *enjoy* getting on with my life. I got up, showered, put in a load of wash, made an appointment to have my hair cut and mopped the kitchen floor.

Major victories! As I moved from task to task, I was aided by a new inner feeling, a positive inner reinforcement that could be gentle and encouraging but at the same time insistent and strong. In the past my inner voice had always been negative, undermining and relentlessly critical. Now I felt a resolve and new sense of purpose that shocked me.

Another Thursday. For over a year the group in Billings had been praying for the woman with the severe problems of addiction. Once again they bowed their heads and said, " 'We know that in everything God works for good with [Sandy] who [loves] him' " (Romans 8:28, RSV).

But at this meeting there was a difference: I was sitting among them.

On a bright June morning in 1979 I walked into a living room filled with smiling women who welcomed me warmly. My neighbor Kathy had invited me, and I perched nervously on the edge of a green sofa, waiting to see what all this "intercessory prayer" was about. I learned for the first time about the prayers that had gone up for me during my darkest days. I still needed much healing, but I was on my way.

Week after week I joined them in their prayers for others and for myself. Then, when I left Billings once again for a treatment center and halfway house, they continued their prayers. And later when I moved to Vermont to start a new life in 1983, I continued to call or write them. Their prayers were making a difference in my life, and I knew it.

Today I am living, breathing proof that prayers for others— intercessory prayers—are one of the most powerful tools that God has placed in our hands. My recovery did not take place in a month, or even a year. It was a long process. Even nowadays, every so often, the tendency toward addictive behavior beckons me back to the old habits. It's then that I say my own prayer: "I, Sandy, can do all things through Christ who strengthens me." Then I bow my head, insert somebody else's name—and pass the prayer along for another.

Prayer Binds Us Together

JANET CHANDLER ESCOTT

When our two-year-old daughter Catherine was rushed to the hospital during a severe asthmatic attack, the doctor warned me that she was very close to death. I paced the hospital corridor, begging God to spare her.

Suddenly, I felt two arms around my shoulders and looked into the motherly face of a Mennonite woman. "I saw them wheel in your daughter," she said. "I've been praying for her. I know God will make her well again."

Her words touched me. "And you, why are *you* here?" I asked.

"My son was hit by a car, and though one of his legs had to be amputated, he survived and is recovering."

How strange. I'd read about that accident in the local newspaper—and had been so moved that I'd knelt and prayed intensely for the youngester. And now here was that boy's mother saying she'd prayed just as hard for *my* child.

Catherine pulled through. And my new friend, Mrs. Shenk, and I both thanked God for showing us the truth of 1 Corinthians 12: We *are* all one body in Christ, and when one member suffers—or rejoices—the whole body does the same.

And prayer is the tie that binds that body together.

Prayer for the Helpless

HELEN INWOOD

Let me be a voice for the speechless,
Those who are small and weak;
Let me speak for all helpless creatures
Who have no power to speak.
I have lifted my heart to heaven
On behalf of the least of these—
The frightened, the homeless, the hungry.
I am voicing their pleas.
If I can help any creature,
Respond to a desperate call,
I will know that my prayer has been answered
By the God who created them all.

Part Three

When It's Hard to Pray

Introduction

Finally, be strong in the Lord and in his mighty power.
. . . And pray in the Spirit on all occasions with all kinds
of prayer.

EPHESIANS 6:10, 18, NIV

Although we may be convinced that prayer is a powerful force
because we are praying to an Almighty God, sometimes praying
is extremely difficult. Those are the times when it is necessary to
give up our own ways, our own point of view, our own will, in
order to enter the flow of God's blessing and power. When we
have been wronged and are asked to forgive the one who
wronged us, when we are shown our true selves and must acknowledge our weaknesses and failures to God, when we come
to the end of our own power and ability and must surrender
everything to God—at these times God asks of us nothing less
than everything, our whole selves.

8.

Prayer That Forgives

Who, Me?

I need to be forgiven, Lord
So many times a day.
So often do I slip and fall,
Be merciful, I pray!
And help me not be critical
When others' faults I see;
For so many times, my Lord,
The same faults are in me.

AUTHOR UNKNOWN

Break-In!

ANNE FITZPATRICK

It had been an especially pleasant evening, celebrating a birthday with old friends. On the way home, my husband Bill and I happily recalled the surprised expressions when the waitress brought the cake with candles, and everyone around us joined in singing "Happy Birthday." All in all it was such a satisfying evening—until we pulled into our driveway.

As soon as Bill raised the garage door it was obvious something was very wrong. The back door to the garage and a porch door stood wide open. I hurried into the kitchen—another open door—and flipped on the light. The door had been broken and split, and the lock chiseled out.

In the living room, papers were strewn all over, and a bookcase door hung askew, pulled off its hinges. Contents of bedroom drawers spilled out into the hallway. Mute testimony to our burglary lay in the discarded metal lockbox we used for daily expense money, bent and misshapen and, of course, empty.

"Oh, no!" I cried. "I don't believe this." As if by denying I could wipe out the unmistakable evidence before us. Things like this happened to other people, strangers in newspaper accounts, not to us!

"Call the police!" Bill said, hurrying past me and going through all the rooms and closets, then the basement, making sure there was no one still in the house. A foolish move, we were told later by the police, but neither of us was thinking very clearly then.

When Bill came back, we surveyed the damage in each room, being careful, as the police had instructed, not to touch anything. My heart beat faster with each discovery of damage and loss, fury and anger locking horns inside me. In our bedroom, personal belongings tumbled over each other on the floor, on the bed; drawers had been pulled out and emptied. My jewelry box had been left on the bed, open; tangled beads, pins and earrings spilled out, left behind, while my few special pieces had been taken.

"The gold heart you gave me for Christmas!" I wailed. "And my little silver cross, the ring from Italy!" I was close to tears, the taste of anger at this violation of our home was bitter in my throat. Bill, speechless, gently squeezed my shoulder.

The police officer arrived and we went through the house again, stepping over and around piles of clothing, papers, books, as he methodically made out a report.

In the bathroom, medicine cabinet contents had been dumped in the sink; it was impossible to tell what pills were missing. We didn't attempt to enter our grown son's room, where piles of his clothes and belongings blocked the doorway—a wild change from Mike's usual order, with never a thing out of place.

Our teenage son's room, never neat, was now a disaster as T-shirts, jeans, books and records formed mountains on the floor and bed. When he came home, incredulous, he declared his losses: several chains and pendants, an engraved silver medal, precious because it was a gift from his girl friend—and nearly fifty dollars, the Prom money he'd been stashing away under his sweaters.

"At least they didn't take my stereo or my guitar," he said philosophically.

"But now they know where they are," Bill said grimly.

His words alarmed me. "You think they'll come back?"

He shrugged. "I hope not."

There was not much sleep that night. Bill braced the broken doors as securely as possible and we made a start at picking up the mess. *The sooner we restore order*, I thought, *the sooner we can begin to put this invasion out of our minds.*

But it was not that easy. I awoke the next morning after dozing uneasily in the last wee hours, feeling bleary-eyed and exhausted—and deeply depressed. I tried to explain it to Bill. "It's not only losing things, and the money—that's bad enough. But I don't feel safe anymore. What kind of people do things like this?"

He shook his head, no more able than I to understand. "But I know what you mean. The biggest thing they've stolen is our sense of security."

Outside the day was bright and sunny. The neighborhood was normal and peaceful as always, contrasting sharply with the chaos we left inside our home as we went to church.

Throughout the service I searched for words of comfort, something to lighten the gloom I felt. There was nothing. I tried to pray, knowing I should begin to let go my anger and forgive. Experimentally I formed the words, but there was no meaning or truth in them.

Back home we talked to shocked neighbors, who shared our sense of outrage. Break-ins were not unheard of in our town, but this was the first on our street and everyone was concerned. The rest of our day was spent completing the cleanup. Mike's room was once again neat and orderly; the only thing missing was a pillowcase. "They probably meant to fill it with cameras, radios, things like that," Bill figured, again raising the question of a recurrence, and another frightening thought: Perhaps we had interrupted them when we came home!

In the days and weeks that followed, Bill worked on repairs, replacing one door entirely and installing new locks. A sense of normalcy returned—except for the creeping fear that had become part of my life. Every time we went out, I compulsively checked and rechecked our new automatic light-timers, making sure the house would look occupied when darkness came. Turning on outside lights. Locking doors, trying them twice.

In the neighborhood, I watched for strangers, looking with suspicion at anyone I didn't recognize. At bridge club, choir practice, in the supermarket, I couldn't stop talking about it; I found many whose homes had been entered, acquaintances who shared my sense of violation. My anger remained at the sizzling point when I heard things like, "We got new locks, and they came in a cellar window." Or, "We thought it would be a good idea to have floodlights in our yard, and all it did was light the way for them." The bitter tones I heard matched my feelings perfectly.

They. Them. The enemy. Unseen, unheard, *they* had invaded our community, always a few steps ahead of us, ahead of the police. Was there no way to be safe from *them*, the unknown *they* who had become such an unwelcome part of our lives?

Our son Bill was the first to tire of the almost nightly dinner-table topic as I shared these conversations. One night he suggested we pray for the intruders, along with our blessing before the meal.

The idea startled me. "Pray for *them?* How can you say that, after they took the money you worked so hard for!"

He didn't miss a beat in the methodical loading of his plate as he explained: "We should stop dwelling on what happened to *us.* We lost only *things,* but *they've* lost a lot more. They're out of the grace of God by breaking His Law."

I looked at him with surprise, this towering young man who often caught me unaware with his unexpected bursts of wisdom. Then, though I sensed the truth of his words and gave lip service to his prayer, I still could not let go the anger and resentment that simmered like an ugly stew within me.

One day a friend came to visit, a remarkable lady of over seventy. Gladys was youthful, active and energetic, and she had a deep, shining faith I admired. Her home had been broken into too, so she understood my feelings when we talked about our experience. But this conversation was different from all the others I'd had recently. Gladys seemed somehow untouched in the way other people had been—and as I myself was. I sensed no bitterness or hate in her.

She smiled when I told her this. "That's not what God wants in me. God wants me to forgive—and to keep my trust in Him."

Her words, like my son's, rang with a truth I slowly absorbed as I prayed, for I did continue to pray, until the words that began as cotton on my tongue became real. One day, praying our Lord's own words, it struck me how often I repeated phrases unthinkingly, not really paying heed to their meaning. Now, *forgive us our trespasses, as we forgive those who trespass against us* had a specific meaning for *me*. I didn't have to wonder what to do, for He had already instructed me.

By not giving up when prayer was difficult, and by listening to the prayers of others—a seventeen-year-old boy and a seventy-year-old woman—I found that now I *could* pray: *Father, forgive them, and take away my resentment against them*—and know there was real meaning in my prayer.

We still lock our doors and turn lights on when we go out, but our trust is not totally in these things. Our trust is in the Lord and in His Word.

In Psalm 37, I discovered another prayer that speaks to me: "Be not vexed over evildoers. . . . Trust in the Lord and do good, that you may dwell in the land and enjoy security" (vss. 1, 3, NASB).

The security of being in God's grace.

Strength Twice Over

BRUCE L. JOHNSON

I have fought two incredible battles in my life. Though they were against entirely different adversaries and happened eleven years apart, they were, in a strange way, related.

My first battle was with a man-eating shark. The second was against a deadlier enemy.

The first began on a sunny day in the Bahamas in 1965. I was there on a brief business trip and had decided to take a few hours to catch a little sun on the beach. At the time I was earning my living teaching snorkeling, judo and body building. I had been doing this since World War II when, as heavyweight wrestling champ of the Navy's Third Fleet, I taught combat Rangers survival techniques. Now at the age of thirty-nine, I was in tiptop physical condition—and proud of it.

That afternoon I relaxed on the warm white-sand beach, eyes closed, listening to the sounds of four native children laughing and splashing in the sea. Suddenly, a long harrowing shriek shot me bolt upright. A little girl was thrashing in the water. For only a second I saw her, her red bathing suit in shreds. Then she disappeared. I leaped to my feet and raced toward the surf. A dark dorsal fin knifed toward the other three children.

"Shark! Shark!" I screamed. I spotted a large, pink conch shell in the sand and scooped it up with my left hand as I plunged into the water. I knew that sometimes a shark can be turned away by hitting it on the snout with a club—pounding your hand against its steel-file hide only draws your blood.

I tried to run waist deep in the water, to attract the shark's attention. I grunted with the effort and surged on, but as the shark slid by me toward the children, I made a desperate lunge and the conch shell struck near the shark's tail.

Infuriated, it whirled. For a split second its jaws grabbed at my right arm, but I turned, pulling my arm free. The shark rolled, raking its tough hide across my face, tearing open my lips. I tasted salty blood. Now the shark grabbed at my right arm again just as I drove the conch shell's point deep into its eye, the one vulnerable spot. Startled, the shark released me and I stumbled for shore.

But not fast enough. Suddenly I felt a pull on my right calf. The shark had me. I hopped frantically on my left leg, as the shark dragged me out to sea. I was not aware of the pain as much as the overwhelming viselike pressure of those jaws. My foot slipped from under me and in that last instant of staring wildly into the sky I gulped as much air as I could; then my head went under.

The shark dragged me down, my back and head scraping and bouncing on the sandy bottom. Here, twenty feet down in the crystal water, I could see sand clouds swirling around with each flip of the shark's powerful tail. My eardrums rang with pain, my chest tightened. Once more I tried to slam the shell against the shark's side. This only made it shake the massive head clamped on my leg. Fiery pain went through me.

If I could just get my leg free, I thought. I tried a half sit-up. I grasped the shark's fin with my right hand. Now I was twisted in a seated fetal position. My upright body increased water resistance, slowing us down until the beast stopped. But now I was close again to the shark's jaws. I grasped the shark's snout with one hand and thrust the shell against its lower teeth, trying to pry its mouth open. But nothing happened.

My vision wavered. I knew I couldn't hold my breath much longer. I had only seconds of consciousness left. I couldn't gouge the shark's eyes, for, enraged, it would bite my head or midsection, killing me instantly. Blackness closed in, and I cried out within, *O, God, help me!*

I felt calm. Was this how one felt just before dying?

With a final thrust I dug the conch shell deep into the shark's jaws and wrenched with all my might. They gave a bit! Adrenalin shot through me. I twisted the shell back and forth. Slowly the jaws relaxed. Now! The mouth was open enough to pull out my leg. But at my awkward sitting angle I could not do it without letting go of those jaws.

My impulse was to let them snap, hoping they would chop my foot off and release me. But then, suddenly, miraculously, my leg was free.

Clawing wildly toward the surface, my lungs screaming, I broke into fresh, sweet heavenly air. And that's all I remember. People found me on the beach still "swimming" in the sand. Jabbering excitedly, they told me that I had been underwater for over five minutes.

It took a year for my oozing wounds to heal and before I stopped limping on a severely wrenched knee. All the while I continued to work out with my special exercise program and eventually got my body into athletic shape. Then in December 1976 the second battle began.

I had a stiff neck that bothered me a lot so I went to see a chiropractor, who turned out to be incredibly inept. He had me on a table while he manipulated my neck with his hands.

"That help?" he asked.

"Doesn't seem to," I answered.

"Well, try to relax completely," he said, "and I'll . . ." At that, he suddenly twisted my neck vigorously. The pain that blazed through me was so great that the ceiling light spun crazily. I was nauseous as he helped me down from the table.

"You'll be okay in no time," he assured me, handing me some vitamin tablets he said would ease my condition.

I drove home using only my right arm since my left had lost its coordination.

When my wife Shari, who is a nurse, saw me stagger in our front door, she thought I'd had a stroke. She called an ambulance. At the hospital I groaned in constant pain while I underwent tests. Finally, conferring neurosurgeons determined that the manipulation of my neck had occluded the vertebral artery causing loss of oxygen to the brain. "A brain stem infarction," they said.

I had gone from a healthy, physically strong person to what seemed an invalid in a quick snap of a neck. I'd lost my sense of balance and coordination on my left side. My heart rate, blood pressure and bladder function were affected, and I suffered from choking spells. I had no feeling on my right side when pricked with pins. When standing, the room seemed to spin and I was nauseous.

After two hospitalizations totaling about six weeks, interspersed with painful tests, I had much time to think about the man who had put me in this condition. When I remembered how he nonchalantly handed me those vitamin tablets, anger swelled within me. I had a burning hatred for him, which was unlike me, as I never before carried grudges.

Then I would recall my neurosurgeons' verdict. "If you don't get better in a few months, well . . ." and my anger festered. The "few months" went by, but instead of improving I discovered that now I had double vision. "A delayed result of the brain stem infarction and not unusual," said my doctors. None of them would predict just what permanent brain damage had been done. Only time would tell, but it did not look good.

More weeks dragged by, then months. Depression set in as I tried to cope with my limitations, wearing a black patch over one eye to improve the double vision and a cervical collar to lessen the severe headaches. I had to use a cane because of my loss of balance.

I diligently followed special therapy exercises I had devised, since teaching exercises was my profession. However, my progress was painfully slow.

I avoided mirrors. The sight of the pale, drawn figure with the black eyepatch and neck collar sickened me. And my anger against the man responsible for it never left me.

One day when my vision began to improve, Shari brought me a Bible. She had been patiently waiting until I could read again. She was a deep-believing Christian who had always tried, gently, to make me understand her love for God. But I had never really tried to understand. I was the black belt judo champion, the man who had fought a ten-foot shark—and won. Somehow I'd even forgotten how I cried out to God during that battle. I believed in physical strength, not spiritual.

Now, however, I began to read her Bible and for the first time in my life, God's Word really began to mean something to me.

Soon I began to accompany Shari to a good "Bible believing and preaching" church. At first I found the services a soothing diversion; it was good to be out again and be with friendly people. But as I continued reading the Bible more, I looked forward to church more, until, one day in early April 1978, I walked down our church aisle and accepted Jesus Christ as my Lord and Savior.

By now over a year had passed since my "accident." I was still struggling with exercises, suffering constant headaches and vertigo. My left arm had hardly improved and both legs were still extremely weak. I stayed in bed or in a chair much of the time, still carrying hate for the man who had done this to me. On the night of May 19, 1978, I was lying in bed listening to the radio. Shari had had a very busy day because of a private duty case and was fast asleep beside me. It was a little after ten o'clock and I was listening to *The 700 Club*. The program's host, Pat Robertson, and his guest, Demos Shakarian, head of the Full Gospel Business Men's Fellowship were reading people's prayer requests.

"Here's one from a man in Oregon," said Robertson, who read a letter in which the writer described having the same neck injury as mine.

I felt sorry for this man, and when Robertson said, "Let's pray for this man right now," I forgot about my own condition and lifted up my hands and began praying for the man.

As I did I thought of the Scripture that our pastor had repeated so often: "And when ye stand praying, forgive, if ye have aught against any" (Mark 11:25). It struck me that here I was praying for God's help when I hadn't forgiven the man who had hurt me.

And so, my hands still raised, I relinquished the hatred. "O

Father," I said, "I forgive him because I know You have forgiven him and You have forgiven my sins, too." As I lay there, hot tears on my cheeks, a startling thing happened. My hands, still above my head, suddenly felt as if they'd touched a bare electric wire. It seemed as if a jolt of lightning shot through me. An excruciating pain seared my neck, so intense that, gritting my teeth, I started to get up to get a pain pill. Wincing, I put my feet on the floor and automatically reached for my cane.

Then, as I stood up, I got another shock. The pain was gone! I had no more dizziness! My vertigo had disappeared. For the first time in a year and a half the room was not spinning. I stood transfixed. I wasn't dreaming, for the radio crackled on; the lamp glowed on the bedside table, Shari still peacefully slept.

My legs! They felt strong again. I gingerly walked across the room, testing them. I didn't limp! I stood on one foot and then on the other. I didn't fall!

God . . . could He have . . . ?

Trembling, I had to find out if this was real. I rummaged in the closet, found my jogging shoes, laced them on. Then I slipped out of the house onto our street.

At first I walked cautiously, then gradually quickened my pace. I wasn't even stumbling! Then with renewed confidence I ran. That verse in Isaiah flowed through my mind: "But they that wait upon the Lord shall renew their strength; they shall mount up with wings as eagles; they shall run, and not be weary; and they shall walk, and not faint" (Isaiah 40:31). In long easy strides I loped down the empty street, the cool night air rushing against my face, my legs and body moving rhythmically, painlessly, freely.

After half a mile, I returned to the house, leaping and exulting, eager to share this healing. I woke Shari and her eyes widened; then she, too, was crying in joy. Together we knelt at the bedside and thanked God for His healing.

And so, those were the two monsters I'd fought. I'd battled a shark for my physical life; I'd battled the monster of hate for my soul.

My Father, the Fisherman

PATRICIA ZIMMERMAN

There it was again. As I slowed to a stop at the light on Route 7, in Connecticut, the joy of the day vanished. The same dark feeling slipped over me. It was never far away. "O God," I cried aloud, "You've given me a new life. I have a job, my children, a loving fellowship. Why does this sadness keep coming back?"

The light turned green and as the car in front of me pulled forward, I glanced at its license plate. The number was 309, the street address of my childhood home in Teaneck, New Jersey: 309 Warwick Avenue. The memories rushed in.

A Dutch colonial house. My gentle mother, my older brother Ed, and . . . my father . . .

I heard again my father's booming laugh when he'd come home from his work as a car salesman, his powerful arms lifting me high, his bright gray eyes sparkling. "Here's my Little One!" he'd say. I loved my father then. When I'd bring home a drawing from school, I'd wait breathlessly for his response. His approval was my heaven, his smile a crowning victory. He was a commanding, talented man, champion skeet shooter and chess player, a fine photographer and an ardent fisherman. How he loved fishing!

But then, at sixteen, my parents' marriage split apart. My father left us, and the light of my world went with him. My mother worked through the days and wept through the nights. For me 309 Warwick became a prison of grief. I longed to break free.

Soon Ed left for college and I fled to New York City for the good life, to drink in the glamour of new friends, new parties, new freedom and the swift magic of alcohol. Soon I had everything, a fine husband, children, a home. But it wasn't enough. I continued to drink. The swift magic turned to slow poison, and the freedom I sought in alcohol became a prison with no reprieve. My marriage failed, my world split apart.

Then a God-given fellowship of compassionate people who understood my problem with alcohol led me out of that prison. They taught me to pray for the faith I had lost, and I found it in Jesus, the Christ . . .

The car with the 309 license plate turned off and vanished in the darkness.

Now my mother was gone. Both she and my brother had been dead for years and I'd long ago lost touch with my father.

Your father, came the words, unspoken; but words I seemed to hear. *Heal your relationship with your father*, came the command.

"I can't!" I said, speaking out loud. "I haven't seen him for years, I don't know where he is. He's probably dead by now." I gripped the steering wheel. "And I don't want to see him again, *ever.*"

How many times had I thought about my father. Reading the Bible I'd think of him and get angry. I'd remember the passage in Matthew, where Jesus speaks about fathers and their children. "Or what man of you, if his son asks him . . . for a fish, will give him a serpent?" (7:9, 10 RSV). Well Dad had given me a serpent. "Explain *that* one to me, Lord!"

I remembered the commandment, "Honor your father," and my heart was cold.

Again it came, an insistent order: *You must heal your relationship with your father.*

At my fellowship meeting the time came to reveal my dilemma. "I haven't seen my father in seventeen years," I said. "What could we say to each other after all this time?"

"How old would he be if he is still alive?" a friend asked.

"Oh, in his late seventies."

"Well, then," she said gently, "you might not have much time left."

I recoiled at her answer, but I knew what I had to do.

I phoned a cousin in Albany. After the usual small talk, I finally got around to it. "Do you know anything about my father?" I asked, my throat tightening.

"Well, we know he's living on Long Island with his sister," she said, then added, "Funny thing, Pat; his cousin Vera said he had been asking about you."

With trembling hands I dialed my father's cousin. We hadn't talked in years. She was happy to hear from me but said sadly that my father was in a nursing home on Long Island.

"He's had a second stroke," she said, "and has lost his speech and desire to eat. I'm afraid it's just a matter of time."

When I mentioned going to see him, she said, "Oh, I don't think he'd know you, Patty; he's too far gone."

"Well," I said, "at least I'd like to call the nursing home."

She gave me the number and the nurse who answered confirmed that it was "just a matter of days."

Suddenly, I felt an urgency to see my father, this man who had once meant so much to me. I had a florist wire him a flowering plant. And then, as soon as I could, I drove from Connecticut to Long Island.

When I pulled up in front of the nursing home I was filled with dread. What do you say to someone you haven't seen for seventeen years . . . to someone you've hated for so long?

I walked down the nursing home corridor, my heart pounding as I approached his door. When I stepped into his room I was stunned by what I saw.

There was my father, the once tall sportsman with the booming voice, now a small, hunched figure propped up in a chair. Tubes snaked from a body that shook with tremors. My plant sat on the bureau; it, too, was dying.

I sat down next to him and took a thin, cold hand. My voice choked. "Daddy?"

I looked into his vacant eyes. There was no sign of recognition. His mind was lost somewhere.

I held his shaking hand, and as I sat there, I knew the hate I'd borne him all those years was gone. I thought of how my mother had suffered when she died.

"O Lord," I prayed, "please don't let him suffer."

Squeezing his hand, I said: "Daddy, it's going to be okay. I love you. I love you."

I stood and wrote a note to his sister, giving my phone number, and placed it on the bureau. Then I stepped back to his chair and, laying my hands on his thin shoulders, I prayed: "O God, bless him, please bless him."

When I arrived home late that evening, my son told me the nursing home had called to say my father had been rushed to the hospital. He was dying.

I wept that night. I wept for the lost years we could have been friends, for the hate I had bottled up inside me. I wept for families everywhere who never forgive one another.

At a prayer meeting two days later I spoke out to the Lord: "I offer up my father, who is dying."

Something broke within me at that moment. I felt at last the peace I had longed for. Now the hate was completely gone. I was filled with love for my father.

On Sunday, a week later, there was another phone call from the nursing home on Long Island. "Mrs. Zimmerman?"

"Yes." I dreaded what the nurse was about to tell me. And then a voice, loud and clear.

"Patty?" The voice was familiar, so familiar that I found it difficult to believe.

It was my father!

And he had a list of orders for me! In rapid fire he asked for my address, told me to call his sister, call his friends, send his clothes to the nursing home and then he put the nurse back on the phone.

"We haven't the slightest idea of what happened to him," she said in a bewildered tone. "All we know is that he was dying when he went to the hospital and he came back well. Why, he's walking the halls, talking up a storm to everyone. He even has a chess tournament going on in the day room."

I could hardly control myself from laughing. It was so like him.

"Everyone here calls him Lazarus," the nurse giggled.

Within a few weeks my father had left the nursing home and he and his sister moved to Maine where he began a wonderful new life in an area he had always loved. When I drove up to see him, he told me he had no memory of my visit to the nursing home. "But that was the turning point, Patty," he said. He looked wonderful!

That was the beginning of our new relationship. We never talked about the past; there was no need. It was over. Somehow I knew his feelings, his suffering, his regrets. And I knew he understood mine. God had given us both new lives.

One thing was clear: he was healed not only in body, but in spirit. One year when he was having trouble with shingles, I told him our church group would pray for him. "Thanks, Patty," he chuckled, "I'll know if it's working."

His letters had a robust humor, full of political opinions and stuffed with photographs he took on his many trips across New England. Knowing my love of poetry, he proudly sent me a photo he'd taken of the home of Edwin Arlington Robinson in Gardiner, Maine. And I sent him a book on fishing, as he still was an inveterate fisherman and Maine was proving a paradise.

But I was not prepared for the biggest surprise.

It came in a bulky letter from Dad. In his strong handwriting he excitedly described his eightieth birthday on which he enjoyed "my greatest fishing trip ever . . .

"We caught a lot, Patty," he wrote, "but your old dad was honored with the prize catch of the day, a forty-inch salmon! I've got to believe, Patty," he continued, "that Somebody up there must like me a little bit." A thrill ran through me.

And then, as I unfolded more of the letter, a photograph fell out and I picked it up. It was "the catch of the day."

There in my hand was the glistening salmon in living color.

"Thank You," I whispered. "Just as You promised. He's given me my fish, just as You promised!"

Change of Heart

HELEN A. STRICKLAND

Wronged and wounded by a friend,
I cried to You in prayer;
Asked for justice, stretched my hand
To You. Yours wasn't there.

Wronged and wounded by a friend,
I sought to understand;
Prayed that I might love, forgive.
You reached and took my hand.

9.

Prayer That's Honest

O God of earth and altar,
Bow down and hear our cry;
Our earthly rulers falter,
Our people drift and die;
The walls of gold entomb us,
The swords of scorn divide,
Take not thy thunder from us,
But take away our pride.

G. K. CHESTERTON
(1874–1936)

The Truth Session

IDELLA BODIE

Swallowing hard, I stood at my dormitory window and watched the wind push snow-swirls down the small mountain and over the main campus of Mars Hill Junior College. My deep sighs—so much a part of my life for the past months—made frosty patches on the glass.

A year ago I'd chosen this college north of Asheville, North Carolina, from catalogs in the high school library. The pictures of majestic mountains reaching into hazy skies, the rock walls, and tree-lined, winding roads had appealed to my quiet nature. A shy girl of sixteen and a lover of books, I dreamed of being an English teacher.

Now I ached with homesickness that covered me like the snow I saw closing over the mountain laurel. I'd expected to miss my South Carolina birthplace and my family, but not to be overwhelmed as I was now. Homesickness—real homesickness—is an affliction that can cause deep psychic pain. I was truly suffering.

Several times each week I wrote my mother, pouring out my heartache, struggling not to ask to break our agreement that I would wait until Christmas for my first visit home. Sending me to college was a hardship for my family, and I knew the long bus trip would impose an unnecessary expense. I also knew that if I went home now I would not come back.

Growing up on a farm, the youngest child, had made me an introspective person. I had spent all of my hours away from school in the pasture with its sweet smell of grass, tunnels made by bullace vines, and violets tucked beside cooling streams. I stroked calves and watched piglets root for dinner, wandered in the haylofts and corncribs, and rode horseback. Now I was over two hundred miles from that dear, familiar place, in the midst of strangers. I cried myself to sleep every night.

It was in this dejected state that I turned from the window and trudged off to the bedtime devotions held on each floor of the dorm by a member of the Baptist Student Union. Most of the girls gathered in the room were already dressed in nightgowns or pajamas with their hair in curlers. After Scripture reading and prayers, the group began the usual chitchat, ranging from "secret passions" (boys who were admired and didn't know it) to Christmas vacation plans. I perched on the sidelines thinking, *Oh, if only I can last that long.*

About that time a tall blonde named Sally, whom I recognized as a music major from down the hall, spoke up suddenly. "Say, why don't we have a *truth session?*"

"A what?" several girls asked at one time. Even I found my curiosity piqued.

"We used to do it all the time at slumber parties back home," Sally went on. "Really. A lot of good can come from it if everybody takes it the right way."

Despite some groans, everyone seemed intrigued.

Before we knew it, Sally had us seated in a circle. The idea, she explained, was to go around the circle telling the truth about each person.

"Okay now," she said, "everybody has to agree beforehand not to get upset but to accept what is said in good faith and work on the problem. Just remember," she added, "the truth is meant to be *helpful.*"

Sally started things rolling by saying she already knew that her habit of humming constantly irritated others—and since she had begun to work on that, she preferred the challenge of a different problem.

Then her roommate obliged by telling Sally she talked too much—and that in her estimation humming was better than nonstop chatter.

The tone of friendly banter caught on as the truth-telling went around the circle. The next girl needed to keep her room tidier, another to be more punctual. And, tactfully, each negative comment was prefaced by a compliment.

I felt a flush rising as all eyes focused on me. How had I let myself get into this situation? Wasn't I feeling bad enough already?

"Idella is a beautiful girl . . ." the speaker hesitated. I recognized her as a girl in my psychology class. "But she's selfish."

A fainting feeling began passing down my body in warm waves. *How could she say such a thing? Why, she didn't even know me.*

"You mean *stuck-up,*" somebody else said.

My mind whirred. Numbness spread over me.

"You just think that because she's so reserved," Sally offered good-humoredly. "She's shy, can't you see?"

I don't remember anything else about the episode except

Sally's admonition that no one must ever, ever refer to what went on this night. Only the receiver was to remember.

Back in my room, I flung myself on my bed and lay there staring at the ceiling. How could they say such things? I had never done anything to them. In fact, I had hardly spoken to any of them. *Selfish*, the girl had said, and no one had denied it. Instead, they had made things even worse by saying I was "stuck-up."

All that night I alternately cried and tried to think rationally. Near daybreak I knew what I would do. The circle of truth had made the decision for me. I would leave this school immediately.

Skipping breakfast, I bundled up and headed down toward the registration office. I wanted to be there when it opened to tell the dean of women about my decision.

By the time I reached the administration building I was shivering from the bitter cold. I had been too eager; the offices were not open yet. I hugged my body against the biting wind; I tried pressing myself against a recessed door adjacent to the offices. Then I thought of the little chapel on the other side of the street. It would not be locked and it would be a place out of the cold until the office opened.

In the warmth of the chapel, I looked about. The one narrow window facing east threw a long bar of light across a table with an opened Bible that stood in the center of the room.

Something about the stillness and the serenity of the soft light affected me. Before I knew it, I was on my knees telling God about my resentments and self-pity. "I've tried, Lord," I said. "You know I've tried."

An echo of the words from the night before rang in my ears. *Selfish. Stuck-up.* Was I really like that? I was sure I wasn't. But if I wasn't like that, then what was I really like?

I looked at the open Bible before me, and suddenly the words of Jesus came into my mind: "Ye shall know the truth, and the truth shall make you free" (John 8:32).

The truth shall make you free? What *was* the truth about me? How did I appear to others?

And suddenly I saw it clearly. In truth, I had spent so much time thinking only of myself and my homesickness that I had built a wall around myself that kept friendship out. I had pictured myself as a quiet, shy person who wrote her thoughts in journals, while others saw me as a person too self-centered to share feelings or to offer understanding.

Now, through the candid words of a classmate, the Lord had allowed me a glimpse of this fixation on myself.

As I knelt before the Bible, I felt my loneliness begin to drain away. God had been with me all along. He was waiting for me to make room in my heart for His love, a love that would warm others.

When I came out of the chapel, slivers of sunshine were bouncing off the snow in sparkling light shards. I was already running back up toward my dorm when I realized I'd forgotten all about going by the registration office.

Back in my room, I wrote to my mother. For the first time since leaving home, I did not burden her with my homesickness. I said, "I want you to know how much I appreciate the sacrifices you are making for me to go to college." I spoke of the snow flurries the day before and of my studies.

On the way to my first class, I knocked timidly at the door of my neighbor's room. She yelled, "Come in!" and I stuck my head in to ask if she'd like to study for the psychology test with me.

"You bet," she said with a surprised grin.

Changing was not easy for an insecure sixteen-year-old. But I began to make a conscious effort to get to know the other girls on the hall. When I felt the urge to draw within my shell and remain quiet, I would ask someone a question about herself. Gradually I learned that in sharing with others I pushed away my problem of homesickness.

And every night I breathed a special prayer for knowing the deepest truth of all: that Jesus loves me, and I have a commitment to share that love with others.

How could I be a teacher, like Him, without being willing to give of myself?

How to Do What You Really Want to Do

VIRGINIA LIVELY

I looked at the figures on the bathroom scale in dismay. I had to admit that despite my best intentions, I was continuing to gain weight. I trudged into the living room, pushed some magazines off the couch and sank down in despair. "O Lord," I sighed, "I have tried and tried to lose weight, but I just can't do it on my own. You'll have to help me."

An odd thing happened when I asked for His help. *Virginia, He seemed to say to me as I prayed, you just want to overeat more than you want to lose weight.*

I was startled and defensive, but I had to admit it was true. I often invented reasons for eating. An upsetting phone call, anxiety about a speech I was to give, *anything* seemed to be a good excuse for sending me off to the refrigerator. And eating itself often got out of hand. Instead of stopping at two cookies, I'd eat the whole bag. Now I had to confess that it wasn't just a matter of will power. It was a question of which did I want more: to eat or lose weight?

So I started to say a different prayer: "O Lord, from this moment on help me to truly *want* to lose weight."

It took time, but gradually I found I wasn't thinking about food as much anymore. If ever I'd reach for that refrigerator door handle between meals, I seemed to hear Him saying: *Which do you want more, Virginia, food or a slimmer body?*

Little by little, as I began to lose weight, I started applying that crucial question to other areas of my life. Exercise, for instance. Again, in my prayers to God, He let me see that I'd rather sit and lounge than exercise. And again I confessed that this was so, asking Him to change my desire.

Sure enough, one morning as I stood at my kitchen window, I felt a yearning to go outside. I put my jacket on and walked around the block. I enjoyed it so much that I did it again the next day. The next week, I increased my daily walk to two blocks, then four. On my walks, I liked the feel of the sun and the breeze and the sight of the pretty flower gardens in my neighborhood. I felt alive.

Then I began to notice how cluttered my house was. I had complained about it to myself for years, making some very good excuses. I couldn't get to it because of speaking engagements. I was too busy.

Can you guess what I started to hear from the Lord? *No, Virginia, you don't get to it because you don't want to. You want it just as it is.*

"My word!" I said to myself. "No, I *don't* want a messy house." Again I prayed, "Lord, I know it's Your will that this house be in order. Please help me."

I began to clean house and enjoy it. I started first with the little bedroom I call my office. Then in the storage room I threw out the old paint cans I'd been saving. I even began coming across people I could give things to, things they needed and could use.

And so I've found three essential steps in breaking irksome habits:

1. Confess that you've been doing what you've *wanted* to do, not what you thought you should be doing.

2. Decide what you really want.

3. Pray. Ask the Lord to help you with your true desire. He will enhance that desire, just as He did for me that morning when I looked out the window and felt the longing to go out and take a walk.

The other day, my daughter telephoned me, complaining, "Mother, my house is a mess. I don't know if I'll ever get it straight. These children won't pick up anything, I can't get the laundry done and—"

I stopped her. "Honey, let me tell you about the 'I-wants' . . . ."

The Fallen Bird's Nest

SUE MONK KIDD

It was scarcely midafternoon, yet the doctor's waiting room was dark. Outside, enormous black clouds roiled and rolled. A storm was on the way. From my green chair in the corner, I felt strangely part of it—the peculiar darkness, the impending storm, clouds rumbling like a rockslide. In more ways than one, it seemed things were about to topple.

I'd come here because of a lump in my breast. I'd discovered it myself and naturally I'd gone to the family doctor hoping he would pat my hand and say, "Nothing to it." Instead, he'd sent me here, to a surgeon.

Lump. I turned the word over in my mind. It always rang the same ominous note . . . striking a particular chord buried years before when I'd worked as a nurse. It was a memory I never tampered with. Now it was all coming back with the swiftness of a dream.

But Mrs. Holly was no dream. She was literally the first patient I ever had. She'd had a lump, one that began her long battle with cancer. I cared for her for months. In all that time she never had a visitor. One morning as I brought her breakfast tray, I found her leaning at the window. Against the breaking light her frail little silhouette reminded me of the dark contours of pain and longing that seemed to shape so much of her life.

"Where is God?" she asked, gazing far into the distance as if she might catch His presence vanishing over the horizon.

"Why, He's right here with us," I replied, serving up the answer almost as easily as her meal.

She turned and looked at me intently. "I wonder . . ." she whispered. And at that moment I felt nearly as lost and unconvinced as she did. We never spoke of it again, but the episode always hung unfinished between us, like a puzzle you can't solve or a book you never complete.

I sat by her bed as she died. There were just the two of us. I kept thinking about the question she'd asked that day. Maybe it was my imagination, but I felt as if she was thinking of it too. She was too weak to talk, but near the end she gave me the faintest little smile. Then she closed her eyes and died. All alone, it seemed.

I felt unsettled for weeks afterward. Sometimes my eyes mysteriously filled with tears when I passed her room. "I know she was your first patient," a colleague said. "But you can't get emotionally involved like this." I took her advice. I packed up the hurt and unanswered questions and buried them. All that remained of the experience was a queer little dread that twisted in the pit of my stomach at every mention of the word *lump*. . . .

The nurse's words cut through my thoughts. "Mrs. Kidd, the doctor will see you." I marched after her, trying to shake the old, disquieting memory.

After the exam the surgeon cleared his throat. "We need to take out the lump and get a biopsy," he said.

"Do you think it could be . . . malignant?" I asked.

He smiled gently. "Now, Sue, most lumps turn out to be benign, and I think it's entirely probable yours will be also. But you know I can't make absolute promises."

Surgery was set. I would check into the hospital in a few days.

An odd stillness squeezed the air as I scuffed my shoes across the parking lot. There wasn't a breath of wind. I told myself I had every reason to be hopeful, that Mrs. Holly was just one person, that thousands go through this and come out fine. I told myself

all the reasonable things. But it was not a reasonable moment.
Alone in the car, the little dread turned into a fear that overwhelmed all the logic in the world.

As I pulled into the driveway at home, the first drops broke
from the swollen skies. I spotted my son in the backyard pulling
his bicycle out of the rain. "Hurry, it's already coming down!"
I yelled.

Bob bumped his wheels over the roots of the oak tree, scaring
up a chipmunk that lived in the woodpile. "Will the storm hurt
the chipmunks?" he called.

"They'll be okay."

"How about *them?*" He was gazing into the crook of an oak
limb, at a bird's nest he'd discovered the week before.

Dear God, life was collapsing on my head and my son was
standing in the rain worrying about birds and chipmunks. "Yes,
the entire animal kingdom will be fine!" I practically shouted.
"Now come on!"

The incongruity continued on all evening—small inconse-
quential details going right on as though no threat existed.

Finally, with everyone asleep, I tossed on my pillow, listening
to the rain crash on the roof. Raveled in my thoughts and fears
were old haunting images of Mrs. Holly and traces of the unsettled feeling I'd had after she died. That unfinished business
. . . it made no sense.

Not wanting to wake my husband, I wandered to the den,
where I sank into a chair. Lightning irradiated the panes with
light, illuminating the backyard. For an instant I glimpsed the
oak pitching and swaying in the night. *Nothing is really certain in
this world,* I thought. I drew my knees beneath my chin as the
wind whirred and slapped like helicopter blades in the blackness.
And suddenly Mrs. Holly's question blew out of the storm.
"Where is God?" Only this time it was no longer an echo lost in
the years between us. It was my very own question.

"Where *are* You?" I cried, startled to hear the words coming
from my lips. Even more startled to realize how abandoned I'd
felt since discovering the lump. It wasn't just facing life's uncer-
tainties that seemed so fearful. It was facing them alone, without
God.

Now a door was opening inside me and before I could stop it,
the rest spilled out too. The part I'd never been able to put into
words. "And where were You back then when Mrs. Holly
looked for You?" I whispered. "If You weren't there for *her,* how

do I know You'll be here for *me?*" The awful doubt I'd carried inside for so long trailed off in the shadows.

I felt terrible saying it, almost disloyal. In all my life I'd never blurted out a doubt to God. But there was relief in it too. I went back to bed much lighter, as if a clean new space had been created inside me.

The next morning a bit of sunshine dribbled over a cloud. The children scurried out to play. It wasn't long before I heard shouts erupting from the backyard. "Mama! Come quick!"

I leaped a row of brown puddles. And there beneath the oak, at the tips of the children's tennis shoes, lay the bird's nest. Sprawled beside it were two newborn birds. They groped in the grass, looking helpless and wet. I looked at them in dismay. Just what I needed.

"They fell from the tree!" cried Bob. "And you said they'd be okay. You said—"

"I know," I interrupted, remembering the branches lashing in the wind.

There was nothing else to do. I knelt down, scooped the hatchlings into my hands and placed them in the nest. But as I knelt over that little scene, it came to me. One small fragment of an old familiar verse. "One of them shall not fall on the ground without your Father" (Matthew 10:29). For a moment I didn't move, as I held the words in my mind and felt them descend slowly into my heart—into a clean, new space, which before had been a closet for my doubt. I could hear God answering the doubts and questions deep inside, answering them in the gentlest sort of way. "I'm here . . . I've been here all along."

I tucked the nest into the ivy that draped the brick fence, while the children agonized over whether their mother would find it. But the next day she appeared on the fence with a beakful of food. The birds were fine.

And I was, too. Just as the doctor predicted, the lump was benign. But just as important, the episode helped me understand something. If God seems far away in the midst of a dark moment, it's not He who's missing, but my ability to perceive Him. And sometimes the way is cleared simply by offering God one's doubts with a gentle honesty.

Somehow I think that's how it happened for Mrs. Holly. For, as that old memory began to heal inside me, I grew sure she'd found the assurance of God's presence. In fact, I wonder if that faint smile she gave me before she died was meant to tell me so. Yes, I think she knew, just as I do now. No one is alone.

Out of the Sky

STEVE DAVIS

Visibility was less than marginal the afternoon of November 17, 1976. Not one of us sitting around the flight business office at Hunt's Airport in Portland, Texas, would have bet more than a dollar that a plane could get through to land. No one counted on the little Cessna 172 that came barreling out of a sky as dark and choppy as lentil soup. And I couldn't have imagined how it would change my life forever.

I'd awakened that morning feeling pretty pleased with myself. One year before, when I'd arrived from North Carolina, my life savings easily fit into my pocket. But now, at twenty-three, I had it made—or so I thought. I was a flight instructor with my own thriving flight school, and three airplanes of my own. One of my first Texas students had been a beautiful young woman named Linda Peters, who was now my girlfriend. I had more money than I needed. That day I was so self-satisfied that I didn't even mind that it was too cold and rainy to do any flight instructing. "Northers" often hit southern Texas, but they blow on through within a couple of days.

Bad weather for flight instructing is perfect weather for indulging in a little "hangar flying." So I pulled on my bomber jacket and drove over to the Chicken Shack to pick up lunch for the boys—Jess, the retiree who did our books; Ray; and A.A., who in his sixties was finally learning to fly. By the time I got back it was drizzling and so foggy I couldn't even make out Corpus Christi across the bay. Only instrument-rated pilots could fly in this weather, and they'd have to fly into the bigger, tower-controlled Corpus Christi International.

But inside, the atmosphere was convivial. I put out the chicken, and we all sat around on the fraying vinyl furniture and jawed a bit, telling tall tales and patching the world's woes. Jess and Ray went on ribbing A.A. for taking up flying so late in life.

"Well, better late than never," A.A. said. "Not like Steve. To hear him tell it, he could fly before he could walk."

"That's right," I agreed. "My mom and dad said the only time I'd sit still was in an airplane with them." And I told them how I'd spent most of my childhood in Mexico, where my dad had been a missionary pilot. As I talked I could see myself as a ten-year-old in shirtsleeves, riding along dusty roads with my dad to the airstrip outside of Guadalajara. How often I'd pictured turning the corner and rumbling up to the most beautiful sight in the world—our Fairchild 24. A hunk of junk, really, an old tail-dragger my dad bought for $300. He'd hung a radial engine in it—an old round one with lots of horsepower. Nice and noisy.

"Let's load'er up, Steve!" Dad would call, and we'd put in as many crates of supplies as the plane could carry. Then we'd strap in. There wasn't a takeoff that didn't scare—and thrill—me to the bottom of my sandals. Then we'd be up in the open skies, flying over villages and rain forests and mountain ranges. "I think I'll take a few winks, Steve. Hold'er steady," Dad would say, and he'd doze off—or pretend to—while I held course and altitude. Then he'd set her down in some mountaintop village that had been waiting for the supplies we were bringing.

The guys grunted their appreciation of the scene and I quit talking. But there was something there, in my past, that was gnawing at me, and had been for the past few months. As the others went on talking, I mentally stayed behind in that mountaintop village.

After we unloaded the supplies, Dad would gather the natives around, and tell them about *Jesus Cristo, El Salvador*. I soaked up every word. Jesus Christ had been intensely real to me then. I even thought of myself as a missionary, and all I wanted to do was to grow up and be a man like Nate Saint, a pilot I'd read about in a book my parents had given me. The book was *Through Gates of Splendor* by Elisabeth Elliot (New York: Harper & Row, 1961). It was the story of five missionaries, including Mrs. Elliot's husband, who were martyred by Indians in Ecuador in 1956. It was a moving story of faith and adventure, but the part I almost committed to memory was about my hero, Nate Saint, the young pilot who flew them on their missions. I admired him so much that when I held course for my dad, I'd imagine I *was* Nate Saint, flying much-needed supplies to remote corners of the jungle. Soon, it *would* be me!

Just the memory of that time brought a catch to my throat. I'd been so joyful, so confident of God. I'd had a faith like Nate Saint's, worth risking everything for. But somewhere along the line . . . what had happened to it? I lived in the adult world now, a world of doubts and conflicts and temptations. Since there was no one around to help me deal with these nagging doubts, I found it much easier to ignore them. So I had quit worrying about Christianity and devoted all my attention to flying. But where my faith once had been, there was now a profound sense of loss. I felt empty inside.

Recently I'd come across my old copy of *Through Gates of Splendor*. I'd tried to put the book away, but I couldn't shake the sadness that gripped me—because of Nate's death, because of my own loss of faith. Finally I stopped and said the first prayer I'd said in years: "Now, wait a minute, God. Something tells me You're not real. I'd really like to know You the way I thought I did. I want to have the faith I used to have. But I just can't blindly accept that stuff I grew up with. If You'll let me know that You're real, I will serve You, but I've got to know. I can't pretend."

I didn't feel any answer to my prayer. In fact, I didn't feel anything at all. And that made me angry.

No, I'd thought, *it's all a farce. My boyhood hero, Nate Saint, wasted his life. He died for nothing.*

The book had fallen open to the photo section, and I'd looked at the picture of Nate's son, Steve, then five years old. *That kid would probably be about my age now,* I'd figured. *And if the truth be known, he's probably in worse shape spiritually today than I am.*

In disgust and anger I'd put the book away. Now, sitting in the flight business office on this stormy day, I was still angry.

I tried to shake those thoughts and get back into the conversation. Wouldn't the guys laugh if they knew I'd been asking for proof from a nonexistent God—and that I was all torn up because no answer was forthcoming?

"Wa-a-ll, we might as well close up," said Jess. "The rain's only getting worse."

As we all stood to start closing, Julio, one of Mr. Hunt's workers, stopped in. He liked to talk with me, because I was one of the few folks around who was fluent in Spanish, his native tongue. "*Hola,* Steve," he said. "*Aquí viene un avión loco.*"

We looked out through the rain, and sure enough, a little Cessna 172 was dropping out of the sky toward the airstrip.

"Nice day for a little scud-running," laughed A.A. But we all breathed a sigh of relief when the plane touched down safely and taxied in.

"Probably drug runners," decided Ray. "What other business would have you out flying on a day like this?"

A few minutes later the pilot and the passenger swung the door open and came in, dripping. They were both young and clean-cut.

"Hello," the pilot started. "We barely made it in. I'm not instrument rated—I didn't think I was going to find an uncontrolled airport. Can we tie down? Is there a motel in town where we can stay and wait for better weather?"

"We're just closing," said Jess. "But yeah, you can tie down." A.A. and Ray were already heading out.

"There's a motel in Portland," I said. "If you hurry up, I'll wait and drive you over." I turned back to Julio to continue our conversation about the weather. *"Este tiempo esta malo."*

"Y peligroso, tambien," agreed the pilot. *"Yo no débía haber volado el avión con un dia como este* [I had no business flying on a day like this]."

The three of us had talked for a few minutes before I realized how odd it was that the pilot, a blond, blue-eyed Anglo, was speaking fluent Spanish. "Where'd he learn the language?" I asked.

"My parents were missionaries in Ecuador," he said. "I grew up there."

"Really?" I asked. "Did you ever hear of any of those missionaries who were martyred down there twenty years ago?"

"One of them was his dad," the passenger said.

"Oh, yeah?" I pursued. "What's your name?"

"Steve Saint," he said.

The boy from the book!

All the air went out of me, like I'd been punched in the chest. It was as if God had used that book to kindle my faith as a child, and now, when I had deeper questions, the boy in the book flew out of its pages and stood here before me!

But did he have any faith? Or was this a cruel coincidence?

It was minutes before I found my voice, but when I did, I tried to act nonchalant. "If you guys want to save your motel bill, I live a mile from here. There's a couch you could stay on tonight."

"That would be great," said Steve.

Far into the night I talked with Steve and his friend, Jim. I wanted to find out what had happened to Steve—did he still believe in God?

When I discovered he had a strong relationship with God and that his father's death had *strengthened* his faith, I grilled him mercilessly. Not once did I mention the book or my childhood. Instead, all of my questioning and anger spewed out toward Nate Saint's son. And he quietly answered each accusation with faith. The relief I felt at letting all of this out was enormous. After all these years, I could finally express my doubts, because Steve Saint had a God big enough and real enough to handle them.

The next day the weather cleared. I stood alone on the runway after Steve and Jim took off. Everything at Hunt's Airport was the same—except me. Twenty-four hours after that physical— and spiritual—storm, I knew that God had answered my prayer in the most personal, loving way possible. Again I had a joy inside that even an airplane had never been able to produce.

There's been a change in Linda's life, too; she also has a close relationship with Christ. We were married soon after Steve's visit, and since then have flown many missions to remote, impoverished villages in Mexico and Central America. But as long as I live, I'll never forget that November day after Steve Saint took off, when I gazed again into the sky—the sky my prayer had sailed through, the sky my dad and Nate Saint and I had flown through, the sky out of which that little Cessna had come barreling. And I knew that through that sky, over the horizon in Mexico and Central America, hungry villages waited for someone like Nate Saint—or me—to fly in with food, and a faith worth risking everything for. And, thanks to God, that faith again was mine.

Prayer

FRANÇOIS FÉNELON (1651–1715)

Lord, I know not what I ought to ask of Thee;
Thou only knowest what I need;
Thou lovest me better than I know how to love myself.
O Father,
give to Thy child that which he knows not how to ask.

10.

Prayer at the End of the Rope

O Lord,
never suffer us to think
that we can stand by ourselves,
and not need Thee.

JOHN DONNE
(1572–1631)

The Prayer of Helplessness

CATHERINE MARSHALL

When I lived in the nation's Capital, I used to notice how often the Washington papers reported suicide leaps from the Calvert Street bridge. In fact, this happens so repeatedly that the site is often called "suicide bridge."

Sensing the human drama behind these brief notices—like the plunge of the young wife who had inoperable cancer, or that of the elderly man whose wife had just died—I often thought that if I could speak with such persons at the zero hour, I would try to stop them with the thought that helplessness is one of the greatest assets a human being can have.

For I believe that the old cliché "God helps those who help themselves" is not only misleading, but often dead wrong. My most spectacular answers to prayers have come when I could do nothing at all for myself.

The Psalmist says, "When I was hemmed in, thou hast freed me often" (Psalm 4:1, Moffatt). Gradually I have learned to recognize this hemming-in as one of God's most loving devices for teaching us that He is real and gloriously adequate for our problems.

One such experience occurred during the writing of my first book. As the young widow of Peter Marshall, Chaplain of the Senate, I was attempting what many felt was the rather audacious project of writing his biography. About midway in the manuscript, I received devastating criticism from one whose judgment I trusted. His words "You haven't even begun to get inside the man Peter Marshall" brought home to me the fact that unless God wrote this book through me, it would be a failure. The realization of my inadequacy as a writer was not only an intellectual one. It was also emotional; there were plenty of tears.

In my helplessness, there was no alternative but to put the project into God's hands. I prayed that A Man Called Peter be His book, and that the results be all His too.

And they were. I still regard as incredible the fact that I hear from time to time of lives changed through a book; of men entering the ministry through the inspiration of Peter Marshall's life.

More recently I saw the prayer of helplessness work in an everyday type situation—the matter of household help. Before my marriage to Leonard LeSourd in the fall of 1959, I was full of trepidation at the thought of taking on the care of three young children. My son Peter John had been away at school for over three years, and I had involved myself with a writing career. In his efforts to reassure me, Len was blithe with promises of household help.

But the help situation in Chappaqua proved unbelievably tight. Months passed. One woman stayed a few weeks, then left. We tried the Help Columns without success; persistent prayer brought us no nearer a solution. I finally decided I would have to do it all myself, but soon found it was more than a full-time job just running a lively household, not to mention my writing commitments.

So—once again the old familiar pattern . . . the prayer of helplessness . . . the admission that I could not do everything myself . . . then the insight that my main responsibility was to our home. If God wanted me to resume my writing, He would show me the way.

After that admission of helplessness, Lucy Arsenault was sent to us—Lucy—steady, reliable, loyal, a jewel of a cook, a jewel of a person.

Why would God insist on helplessness as a prerequisite to answered prayer? One reason may be because our human helplessness is bedrock fact. Where God is left out of one's life, self-sufficiency is a complete delusion.

What is the truth? Not one of us had anything to do with his being born; no control over whether he is male or female, Japanese or Russian or American, white or yellow or black. Nor can we influence our ancestry, nor our basic mental or physical equipment.

After we are born, an autonomic nervous system controls every vital function that sustains life. A power that no one really understands keeps our heart beating, our lungs breathing, our blood circulating, our body temperature up.

A surgeon can cut tissues, but he is helpless to force the body to bind the severed tissue together again.

We grow old relentlessly and automatically.

Self-sufficient? Hardly!

And the planet on which we live . . . we are helpless there too. The little planet Earth is exactly the right distance—some 92 million miles—from the source of its heat and light. Any nearer, and we would be consumed with solar radiation; any further and we would be frozen to death. The balance of oxygen and nitrogen in the air we breathe is exactly right. The law of gravity operates. And man—little man who struts and fumes upon the earth—self-sufficient? Not at all . . .

Did Jesus have any comment to make about all this? Yes, He put His finger on the heart of the matter as always: "Without me ye can do nothing," He said (John 15:5).

The setting for this sweeping statement by Jesus is the 15th chapter of John: "I am the true vine . . . ye are the branches" (vss. 1, 5).

Dr. Arthur Gossip, who wrote the exposition on John for the famous Interpreter's Bible (Nashville: Abingdon Press) has this interesting comment: "These are surely the most hopeful words in Scripture . . . *Apart from me, ye can do nothing.* For it is on the basis of that frank recognition of our utter fecklessness, apart from Him, that Christ . . . gives us His great promises."

Helplessness? Utter fecklessness? Most of us do not enjoy admitting it. The cult of humanism in our day has trained us to believe that we are quite adequate to control our environment and to be masters of our own destiny.

Yet sometime in life, every one of us finds ourself caught in circumstances that we are helpless to change. So in our physical world, and in our spiritual life, the scriptural statement is true: "A man can receive nothing, except it be given him from heaven" (John 3:27). He must have meant that an omnipotent, trancendent, and imminent God is above all and through all far more completely than we realize.

I have always been impressed by the story of Dr. A. B. Simpson, a famous New York preacher. Poor health had haunted this man. Two nervous breakdowns plus a heart condition led a famous New York physician to tell him that his days were numbered. Simpson was then only thirty-eight.

The physician's diagnosis only underscored the physical helplessness that the minister knew only too well. . . . Always he preached with great effort. Climbing stairs or even a slight elevation was a suffocating agony of breathlessness.

It was at Old Orchard, Maine, that Dr. Simpson attended a unique religious service which sent him back to his Bible to find out for himself about Christ's attitude towards disease. He became convinced that Jesus had always meant healing to be a part of His gospel for the redemption of total being.

Soon after this revelation, Dr. Simpson took a walk. Coming

to a pine woods, he sat down on a log to rest. Soon he found himself praying, telling God of his complete helplessness with regard to his physical condition. He then asked Christ to enter him and to become his physical life for all the needs of his body, until his lifework was done.

"There in the woods, I made a connection with God," he said later. "Every fiber in me was tingling with the sense of God's presence."

A few days after that, Simpson climbed a mountain three thousand feet high. "When I reached the top," he related joyfully, "the world of weakness and fear was lying at my feet. From that time I had literally a new heart in my breast."

And so he did. For the rest of his life, he was noted for the amazing volume of his pastoral, and literary work. He lived to be seventy-six.

Now why does the prayer of helplessness work this way? Because trouble can be the starting point for both spiritual power and creativity. Creativity may be defined as the ability to combine old means into some new form. It is only when old ways of doing things are forcibly broken up by need or suffering that we are compelled to rethink, to begin again. Then the creative process begins to flow.

Fritz Kunkel, the eminent psychologist, puts it like this in his book *How Character Develops*, written with Roy Dickerson (New York: Scribners, 1940, pp. 131–32):

"The way to real creativeness is through danger or suffering. . . . He who . . . relies upon his own small private consciousness must fail, for the source of creativity is not the individual but the We, or to state it another way, the God who manifests Himself in the We. . . ."

To one beset by difficulty and discouragement, here are three suggestions for finding help through the prayer of helplessness.

First, be honest with God. Tell Him that you are aware of the fact that in His eyes you are helpless. Give God permission to make you feel your helplessness *at the emotional level*, if that's what He wants. And recognize that this may be painful. There is good psychological reason why this first step is necessary. Unless the power of our emotions is touched, it is as if a fuse remains unlit.

Second, take your heart's desire to God. You have accepted your helplessness. Now grip with equal strength of will your belief that God can do through you what you cannot. It may seem to you for a time that you are relying on emptiness, dangling over a chasm. Disregard these feelings, and quietly thank God that He is working things out.

Third, watch now for opening doors and opportunities for creativity. When the right door opens, you will have a quiet inner assurance that God's hand is on the knob. That is the time of action for you, for the beginning of the most creative period you have ever known.

An Enchanted Place

LINDA ANDERSON

That September morning, I sat in our trailer deep in the mountains of north Georgia, reading to my daughter BJ, who'd stayed home from school with a headache. It was just the two of us. My husband, Boyd, a teacher, had left for work, and our younger children, Annmarie and John, had caught the school bus. I'd planned to work on the log house Boyd and I were building near the trailer, but I was happy to spend the morning with BJ instead.

Born with a rare condition called Rubenstein-Taybi Syndrome, BJ was mentally retarded. At seventeen she had a big smile and an exuberance for life that spilled over to everyone around her. Her physical mobility wasn't restricted. She attended a school for the handicapped. At home she loved to jump happy somersaults on the trampoline beside the trailer. Sometimes I even forgot what the doctors down in Atlanta had told us—that BJ probably wouldn't live past sixteen. It certainly never occurred to me that morning that BJ's headache was anything to worry about.

She leaned back on my shoulder as I turned the pages of her favorite book, *The Secret Garden*. We read about an enchanted place hidden behind an ivy-covered wall and how it transformed the life of a lonely, miserable girl who found it. As the story ended, BJ closed her eyes.

While she napped I gazed through the window at our log house. It had always been my dream to build a home beneath the misting, blue-green mountains I'd known since I was a child. The mountains were part of me, sure as my hands and feet. They cradled memories of Daddy playing "Red Wing" on his fiddle, midwife Fanny Wilson hurrying to deliver a baby, and folks praying on their knees in the little mountain church. But mostly the mountains reminded me of the old tenant house where I'd lived as a child. I remembered clear as yesterday the room with the glowing potbellied stove, the smell of sage drying on the wall, and the stick on Mama's butter churn making music.

But there were hard memories too. Mama had gone to work as a maid to feed us children after Daddy died. She'd even taken in ironing at night and gone hungry so we could eat. I marveled at how she'd handled so much hardship, and I'd been inclined to chalk it up to her own indomitable spirit. But Mama had believed it was God who saw her through. "When difficulties come, you only have to call out to God and He'll be right there helping you," she always told me.

As the old memories drifted away, I turned from the window and found BJ waking up. She stood and walked down the hall of the trailer toward the bathroom. I watched with a small, perplexed frown. She was walking strangely, swaying, wobbling. Yet before I could move, before I could draw another breath, BJ fell to the floor.

Her body jerked with a violent convulsion. I was a licensed practical nurse, but there was nothing I could do to stop it. When the seizure finally subsided, BJ was unconscious, and nothing in our lives would ever be the same again.

The doctor told Boyd and me she'd had a terrible stroke and the damage to her brain was permanent. She would live, but she wouldn't talk or walk or do anything ever again. Because of my nurse's training, the doctor suggested I care for her at home, and that was the only way Boyd and I wanted it. Besides, there was no way we could afford anything else, even with Boyd teaching a full schedule of electronics classes at North Georgia Technical School. The medical bills were already staggering, especially with the debt on our log house.

It wasn't quite complete, but we moved into the house so BJ could have a big room of her own. And it was there I began my endless vigils by her bed. She had to have care every minute, to be fed, changed and bathed. It took hours to spoon liquid food into her mouth because of her tendency to choke. But worst of all were the seizures.

BJ suffered one or two convulsions a day, and sometimes so many I stopped counting. Each time one came I gave her the injection prescribed by the doctor and fought to keep her breathing. When it was over, she lay so still and blue that I would touch her heart to see if she was still alive.

Caring for BJ became the only world I knew. I wasn't able to leave the house even to go to the barn. I saw the mountains only from the windows, and gradually I stopped seeing them at all. BJ became more and more of a burden. Inside I ached for the laughing girl who bounced on the trampoline and burrowed her head against my shoulder while we read *The Secret Garden*. But that girl was gone forever.

Meanwhile the bills mounted. I put hand-me-downs on the children, and Boyd raised vegetables in the garden and took a second job. Thank goodness most of our creditors were like the man at the hardware store, who said he'd wait till we could pay him back. It seemed to me he would be waiting forever.

As the months dragged by I dwindled to ninety-eight pounds, with raccoon circles under my eyes; my spirit withered. Finally one winter night more than two years after BJ's stroke, I reached the absolute end of my strength. It was 2:00 A.M. and BJ was caught in the grip of a convulsion that seemed to go on forever. When it ended I placed the oxygen mask over her face to draw the color of life back into her, then sank into a chair, lower than I'd ever been in my life. I'd tried to manage by myself, but I knew I could not go on. *What am I gonna do?* I thought. I cried like a child. And suddenly I found myself thinking about Mama, about her simple belief that God would come and help in difficulty if only we called on Him.

Utterly helpless, I fell on my knees and began to pray, feeling the words come from a place so deep inside of me that it seemed to have no bottom. "Dearest God, I need You," I cried. "I accept the difficulty life has handed me. But please, help me. Just send me some way to cope with it."

The moon's light was streaming through the window. I watched it, a downy sort of light, and a soft feeling of peace stole over me. In my mind I saw God bending over me and BJ as if we were two chicks.

The next morning I rubbed the sleep out of my eyes and peered out BJ's window. Everything seemed dipped in a kind of radiance. Pine trees appeared to my eyes like cones of the greenest green I'd ever seen. I looked down at the brown heart of a sunflower near the porch, noticing the way it spiraled like a staircase. I was seeing shapes and intricacies I'd never noticed before. Colors seemed brighter, images more vivid. I knew God had come in the night and unveiled my eyes! I shook my head, bewildered by what it meant.

"Something good's gonna happen," I told Boyd at the breakfast table. The flicker of faith I'd felt the night before had ignited into an overpowering anticipation that God was somehow going to answer my prayer for a way to cope. Boyd smiled. It was the first hope he'd seen in me in months.

A week later my sister, Barbara, came to visit. She found me by BJ's bed looking through the window. "Why don't you paint a picture?" she said out of the blue.

"Paint a picture?" I'd never painted anything but the faces on some dolls I'd made once.

"Why not?" Barbara said. "I'll bring you some canvases. Just promise me you'll paint something you know about."

I thought about the mysterious gift of seeing that had come to me in the night, and somehow I knew my sister's voice was really God's. *Paint a picture*, He was saying.

"I could paint what I love," I said, thinking about my life in the mountains, about the little mountain church, about Daddy and his fiddle, and Mama beating out a rhythm on her butter churn.

Suddenly pictures were flashing in my head bolder and faster than I could take them in. I was seeing them the way I'd seen the pine trees and the sunflower from BJ's window. I was seeing them with some kind of holy fire in my eyes.

The next day as I sat with BJ, I propped a seventy-nine-cent canvas atop my lap and began to paint. I painted the room of my childhood: the black wood stove glowing with a red light, sage drying on the wall, the old butcher-block table laden with molded butter. In the center I painted Mama at her butter churn, and in the corner, a window with snow falling hard outside.

From time to time I looked up from the canvas to BJ, mystified by what was happening. For the more I painted, the more I seemed to be inside that room, drawing up warmth and quietness and love. And it came to me: that room was really a place inside my own heart, a transforming place like the secret garden in BJ's storybook. I knew that through this gift of painting, God was giving me a refuge where I could find the peace and strength to cope with the harshness on the outside.

Through the spring and summer I painted mountain images by BJ's bed, and every day I felt myself gaining new strength. I began

to find peace in caring for BJ, thanking God for the things He
allowed me to do for her.

By summer's end something wondrous was happening to BJ
too. Gradually she began taking most of her meals without choking. And one day the seizures simply stopped. Her cheeks grew
pink as rose petals. She was still inside her own silent world, but
I could tell by her face that BJ was finally at peace.

Her improvement allowed me to get out some. As Labor Day
approached, a friend called and invited me to participate in an
arts-and-crafts show in Homer, the Banks County seat. "You
could sell some of those dolls you made," she suggested.

I agreed, hoping I could sell enough to buy school shoes for the
children. But after I hung up, an unexpected idea sparked in my
head: *Take your paintings.* The thought came again and again.

So on the day of the show, Boyd carted more than twenty of
my pictures over in his old truck. I set them out, wondering if the
$35 I was asking was too much. Then I bent over my easel to
finish one more painting to add to the others.

"Hello, I'm Dr. Burrison from Atlanta," a voice behind me
said. "And I don't think you're asking a fair price."

My throat went dry from embarrassment as I turned to find a
distinguished-looking man studying my pictures. "Well, I didn't
rightly know what to ask," I said apologetically.

"Oh, no," he said. "You should be asking a lot more."

He was, it seemed, a specialist in folk art, and he wanted to give
my name to an art dealer in Atlanta. I think that astonished me
even more than what happened right afterward: a woman came
by and bought every single painting I had—even the half-finished
one on the easel.

True to his word, Dr. Burrison contacted the art dealer, and
less than a year later I was having a real art show at the Alexander
Gallery in Atlanta. Amazingly, it was a sellout, and since then
other shows have followed. And the thing I thought would never
happen did—we paid back the man at the hardware store and
began to put our financial burdens behind us.

Today I have a whole new life. I paint near BJ's bed, caring for
her as always. But she is no longer a burden; she is a joy. Most
important, I have learned a simple truth, one Mama knew all
along: that there is no difficulty so big or so dark that God cannot
help us find a way to deal with it. His strong peace is hidden away

in the most unlikely places in our lives. And if we ask, He will come and set it free to sing inside us like the music of a butter churn.

The Marvelous Calf-Rope Principle

DOROTHY SHELLENBERGER

My husband Charles and I were driving my Uncle Frank, age eighty-five, arthritic old saint, lovable as a puppy, stubborn as a mule, and deaf as a post, back to his Oklahoma farm. The three of us had shared a near-perfect two-week holiday in Colorado.

It was Father's Day. Our plan was to drop Uncle Frank at his old homestead outside Oklahoma City and then make it back to our home in Waco, Texas, where our four grown children and their families would join us for dinner.

We had stopped to call Clara, the woman who cooked meals and took care of Uncle Frank, to ask if she would mind preparing a light lunch for the three of us. But a woman I didn't know had answered. After much hemming and hawing, she informed me that Clara had suddenly married an old sweetheart and departed. "Ma'am," the woman said, "I don't know nothin' else. Clara asked me to come in this morning and feed the animals. She left you all a note."

Uncle Frank and Charles were waiting in the car when I came outside. I crawled in the back seat feeling like someone had socked me in the stomach. Charles turned questioning eyes in my direction, but I silenced him with a shake of my head and an uplifted palm.

"Will Clara fix some of my gen-u-wine garden tomatoes for lunch?" Uncle Frank asked, completely unaware that anything was wrong.

"I forgot to ask," I mumbled.

How was I going to break the news? How would my old uncle, so crippled with arthritis he could hardly walk, manage without Clara on whom he had depended for years? As the miles melted behind us, I weighed alternatives.

I couldn't put him in a nursing home, even temporarily. In his delirium following major hip surgery three years ago he kept repeating, "Girl, you won't put me in a rest home, will you?"

When finally he was fully conscious, I had promised, "Uncle Frank, unless the day should come when you wouldn't know the difference anyway, I give you my solemn word that I will never put you in a rest home."

Moving him to Waco to live with us wasn't a satisfactory alternative either. For years Uncle Frank had lived with his sister, my mother. When Mother died, we had offered to recreate his den and bedroom in our empty boys' room.

"Can I bring Blanche and Julie and Kate and Martha and Bess and Annie?" he asked mischievously, naming his registered Holstein cows. "And can I bring Dot?" Dot was his Border Collie dog named after me. "How about my chickens on your city lot? No, girl, if the day ever comes that I have to move away from all my old friends, both two-legged and four-legged, I hope it is my last . . . I pray to God every night He'll let me stay right here till the day I die."

Uprooting Uncle Frank was not the answer.

Miles back, Charles had turned on the car radio, but now Uncle Frank interrupted its drone. "Boy" (we had grandchildren, but Charles was still "boy" to him), "turn off that blasted radio. Dorothy hasn't spoken one word since she called Clara. Something's wrong. Has anythin' happened to Dot?" Dot was getting old, too.

Then, I had to tell him the whole story—that Clara was gone.

His voice was almost a whisper. "No wonder she wanted me to come on this trip so much." . . . Twenty miles later, "She ironed up all my shirts . . . said I had enough to last a year." . . . Another fifteen miles . . . "Did you notice she gave me a little peck on the cheek when we left? She's never done that before. She was plannin' on leavin'."

By the time we reached El Reno, Uncle Frank had dozed off, and Charles and I talked. He said I should stay with Uncle Frank and try to find a housekeeper. He would go on home to be with the children and grandchildren on Father's Day. "It's not going to be easy finding someone who will be conscientious about staying with an eighty-five-year-old man," he said.

"I've got a few aces up my sleeve," I said. "Maybe it won't be too difficult."

"I'll be praying for you, dear."

"Okay, honey, you do the praying and I'll do the work," I answered glibly.

An hour later, Uncle Frank was having a loving reunion with his Border Collie dog and his big cat "Tom." He ate the lunch I prepared and limped out to look over his beloved land.

I kissed Charles good-bye and reassured him I'd be home in a few days.

Monday morning I called the church where Uncle Frank had worshiped for fifty years. The associate pastor came over with the entire church roll; together we looked for a widowed lady who might like to have a relatively easy job with good pay and a snug little home in the guest house. We didn't come up with one interested person.

Tuesday morning I went to nearby Yukon, a Czech community where Uncle Frank had done business for as long as I could remember. Today it is a major extension of Oklahoma City, and the "good Czech people" who had once saved their money were now enjoying spending it. All the thrifty widows I had envisioned hiring were off on summer tours of Europe.

Wednesday I stayed on the phone all day, calling friends and acquaintances, anyone I thought might give me a lead. "A dependable housekeeper?" one good friend laughed. "Dorothy, you have to be kidding. They disappeared before the miniskirt."

On Thursday I placed a "Help Wanted" ad in the *Daily Oklahoman*.

The ad ran for two weeks and netted two applicants. One never showed up for her appointment. The other was so slovenly I was afraid to let her in.

What was worse, I was beginning to resent Uncle Frank. He was as calm as if my being there were permanent. Every night after puttering around the place all day, he listened to the ten o'clock news, read his Bible for a while and trundled off to bed, falling asleep as soon as his head hit the pillow. I was tossing and turning for hours before dropping off in a restless sleep.

The morning of July 3, we were sitting at the breakfast table. Uncle Frank usually said a simple grace. But this morning he called on me, and suddenly I was pouring out my heart. "Lord," I prayed, "I'm at the end of my rope. I don't know what to do. I can't stay here, and I can't go home. I love Uncle Frank, Lord, but I know You love him more than I do. Would You please take charge here? Thank You. Amen."

When I raised my head, Uncle Frank was smiling. "Well, girl, now that you've learned the calf-rope principle, we can expect a miracle."

"The calf-rope principle?" I asked numbly. "What's that?"

"Dorothy, you know whenever you need to brand a calf or treat it for some disease, you've got to lasso that little critter first. You know he'll run as if you were a coyote wantin' him for supper. It's only when he's reached the end of his rope that you can do what's best for him. Well, girl, it's the same way with the Lord. Long as we want to do things our way, He lets us. When we come to the end of our rope and are willin' for Him to take over, that's when we can depend on Him to do what's best for us. And we can thank Him, too, knowin' He's gonna work it out to His glory and for our good."

"Who taught you the calf-rope principle, Uncle Frank?"

"David did—in the Psalms. He wrote, 'When I was pinned down, You have freed me often.' " (Uncle Frank's interpretation of Psalm 4:1.)

"When did you apply the calf-rope principle to our predicament?" I asked.

"Comin' home, somewhere between Elk City and El Reno."

"Then why is it taking so long to get an answer?"

"The Lord was waitin' on you to learn the principle, too," he said.

Mulling over Uncle Frank's words after breakfast, a name popped into my head. Tom Little.

Tom was the son-in-law of friends of ours in Waco. He and his wife, Becky, and their two boys were living in Oklahoma City when my mother died, but they had moved to Greenville, Texas, shortly afterward. Hadn't Tom recently been transferred back to Oklahoma City? Hadn't I heard that Tom was living in one room because he and Becky hadn't been able to sell their home in Greenville? Hadn't Tom been the one who had said that his dream was to live on a farm like this someday?

A telephone call verified all my questions, and the next day, July 4, Tom and Rebecca Little and their two teenage boys, Tommy and Bruce, drove up from Texas to see us. Nothing was said to Uncle Frank about their coming. They just dropped by for a friendly visit "since they were in town for the Fourth." But when they left I just knew that they were coming back.

"Uncle Frank," I said, picking up the empty lemonade glasses in his den, "what would you think about sharing this big house with the Littles? Tom was raised on a farm. Becky is a good cook. You would have your den and bath and bedroom and join them for meals. The boys seem so courteous and cheerful. What do you think?"

Uncle Frank turned his blue eyes to meet mine. "Dorothy," he paused a long time, "sometimes this past year, I've been so lonesome in this big empty house, I've turned the radio up just to keep me company. Clara has been bringin' my meals in since your mother died. I've eaten alone for the past year . . . Did you hear Bruce askin' me about the Oklahoma Run? . . . Tommy plays the guitar—that's my favorite. I'm sure willin' to give it a try if they are. When can they move in?"

Through tears I said, "Next week."

I'd never realized how lonesome Uncle Frank had been since my mother's death.

The Little family gave Uncle Frank two of the happiest years of his life. He died in October 1972, but, they are still there eight years later, taking care of the old home place that he loved so much, the house where Uncle Frank lived out every day of his full life and taught others how to live by the principles of the Word.

A Letter from Death Row

ANNE PURDY

Our home is in a truly isolated gold region of northern Alaska, up a two-hundred-mile stretch of mountainous road. There is no school, no church.

For ten years I taught school classes gratis in my house to Indian, Eskimo and Caucasian children. Living conditions were intolerable for some of them. Having a big house and no children, we adopted ten and raised them as our own.

But there were others who needed help and there wasn't much we could do for some of these.

One boy, William Albert Tahl, used to come to our house whenever he was upset with troubles at home. Art, as he was called, would stay with us for a few days until things quieted down and then he'd go home. Art first came to us when he was eleven but he returned often through the years. We tried to help with school lessons, clothes, food, outings and provide him with love.

But Art had deep wounds inside that love could not heal. Late in his teens Art left home for good, and for years I did not hear from him. Then I received the following letter:

Dear Teacher:

Perhaps you don't even remember me from your class-room and home over fifteen years ago. I remember you so very well. It's a long, ugly story, but I won't bother you with details.

I am in Death Row awaiting execution. In a drunken rage I committed murder. I deserve to die and it's okay, but one thing bothers me. I'm afraid of what comes after death. I know you believe in God and prayer and that is why I ask your help now.

In other words, I cannot face what lies beyond with guilt on my soul and no hope of forgiveness. If you still believe in God, write and give me the courage to face death.

Your friend, Art Tahl

After reading this letter I sat stunned for a while. How well I remembered the handsome lad with his charming manners and light-hearted disposition despite his troubles.

Taking a day and night to think it over and choosing my words carefully, I wrote Art, assuring him of my friendship and inter-est. In closing I said, "We are forgiven until seventy times seven and Christ died on the cross for the remission of our sins. Re-member He said 'Though your sins be as scarlet, they shall be as white as snow' (Isaiah 1:18). With God all things are possible; you need only to turn to Him."

From the agony of his tortured soul, the condemned man began writing his innermost thoughts and fears. It was almost as though I looked into his heart and understood the sorrow and tribulation written there.

I answered the letters regularly, sending religious cards and poems. I also sent scriptural passages. Art followed my advice and read the Bible daily. Day and night I prayed for him.

As time dragged on for Art, I sensed a gradual change in his spirit. His letters were more hopeful. In one letter he made a remark I'll remember for a long time:

"I've always thought about myself first in everything. There are 58 men due to go to the gas chamber the same as I. Lately I think of and pray for them and I can even smile at the guards and pray for them too. My last act at night and my first when I awake is to pray that God will bless and help all the unfortunate people in the world."

Now was the appointed time for a very special letter. I sat down and wrote to Art without thinking it out; words poured from my pen:

Dear Art:

You are now ready for the great step. Take a large sheet of paper and write down all the crimes of your life, your fears and hopes. Lay all your sins on God's altar. When the lights are out and the guards are gone, get down on your knees and say, "God, here it is, all of it. You need no light for You are the light of the world. Forgive me, Father."

Destroy the paper. Never divulge the contents to anyone. Complete forgiveness, and abiding faith, a cleanliness of mind, body and soul will be given you to last through Eternity.

Anne Purdy

I soon received an answer to my letter.

Dear Teacher:

I followed your instructions perfectly. I want you to know because you love me regardless of everything. I stayed on my knees all night praying. I wasn't conscious of time or anything, only of God's forgiveness and love pouring over my guilty soul.

When the guard came with breakfast I lay on the floor as though dead. The man stared at me, turned white, fear showed in his eyes. "You okay?" he choked out.

I nodded and smiled. The guard looked at me again. "My God," he gasped, "there's a light on your face." He set the tray down and fled.

Through God's grace I am clean, clean. I could shout it from the housetops. Thanks for bringing me to God. I'm not afraid anymore, of death or the hereafter.

I am condemned to die in the gas chamber. I am ready,

God is with me. My body will die but not my soul. All is well, strong and sure. I go forth to meet my God.

Art Tahl

Editor's note: Art Tahl was not executed in 1967, when this story was published, but was finally released in 1987.

Hands

JAMES D. SMITH
U.S. PENITENTIARY, LEAVENWORTH, KANSAS

Hands express many things . . .
Sorrow, gladness, fear.
Hands can push someone away,
Or hold them very near.

Hands create beautiful things
And some hands can destroy.
Hands can spank a naughty child
Or mend his broken toy.

But there's another use for hands,
Which everyone can afford.
And that's when you reach out and say,
"Take my hand, please, Lord."

Part Four

Answers to Prayer

Introduction

I sought the Lord and he answered me.

PSALM 34:4, NIV

Every genuine prayer gives God a chance to work for us. His power is available to keep us going in both boring and difficult circumstances. His healing, as Whittier wrote, "is by our beds of pain." Though healing is one of the most mysterious areas of God's working, these stories give us some clues as to how healing comes. Offering ourselves in prayer for others, giving God all our attention and love on behalf of someone else, searching for the emotional causes for physical illness—these open a way for God's power to work not only for others but for ourselves.

Often we want God to answer our prayers in a specific way—we have a definite idea about *what* the answer should be. But God's thoughts about what we need are often different from ours, and so His answers may come with some shock and surprise. Sometimes they're unexpected because we think we know *how* God will answer. And then there are times when we ask for the wrong things, but God answers our underlying requests. And in the process we discover that God doesn't make mistakes.

11.

Prayer That Sustains

Along the Way

Though life's road is not a smooth one,
   Opportunity still knocks:
God will show us how to fashion
   Stepping-stones of stumbling blocks.

MILDRED N. HOYER

An Elevating Idea

SUSAN STETSON RENAULT

A while back, primarily for financial reasons, I needed to find a job outside the home. A job with a school seemed ideal, since it would allow me to be with my children in the afternoons and during school vacations.

I learned that a new high school would be opening in our district of Colorado Springs and decided that was where I wanted to work. I called the district office constantly—even before the new building was finished—asking for an interview. " 'For I know the plans I have for you,' declares the Lord, 'plans to prosper you and not to harm you, plans to give you hope and a future' " (Jeremiah 29:11, NIV).

My prayers were answered, and I became a receptionist at the brand-new school. It took me about four days to discover that the job bored me to death. I grew exhausted reading newspapers. Wearily I'd watch the clock drag through the hours. I organized my paper clips twenty-one different ways.

One evening I collapsed onto the couch in despair. What could I do? "Then you will call upon me and come and pray to me, and I will listen to you" (Jeremiah 29:12, NIV). God *was* listening, and in His wisdom He reminded me of the elevator man.

Years before, when we lived in Chicago, we took some visitors to the Sears Tower. However, it wasn't the view from the world's tallest building that impressed me most. It was the elevator operator who whisked us up and down those 110 stories. He took a job that must certainly rank among the dullest in the world and made it fun. His friendly humor was contagious as he showed us how to bend our knees in preparation for landing. In a matter of seconds he made our lives a little brighter.

If this man could run an elevator joyfully, I could do the same with the reception desk. The trick was not to dwell on its dullness but to creatively introduce some fun into the job. It shouldn't be too hard, I thought. After all, how could a building with a thousand bright, fun-loving teenagers possibly be dull?

The next day I began a trivia contest by posting a provocative question beside my desk. No fanfare, no announcements—I just waited for students to notice. And when they did, I said, "A sucker for the right answer," having already stashed lollipops in

172

my desk drawer. You'd think I'd offered a pot of gold. Kids raced to the library to learn the name of Australia's president.

My desk soon became a "stopping place," with students coming by first thing each day "to check the question."

I later put puzzles on my desk—a Rubik's Cube or pegboard teasers. During lunch hour or waiting to see an administrator, students would play with the puzzles or just talk to me. I became a sort of mother confessor—a friend.

And to anyone who inquired, "Doesn't your job get boring?" I'd say, "Not at all." And then I'd offer a prayer, thanking God for "elevating" me out of discouragement. Just as it says in Jeremiah 29:13 (NIV): "You will seek me and find me when you seek me with all your heart."

What to Pray For

PHILLIPS BROOKS (1835–1893)

Do not pray for easy lives.
Pray to be stronger men.
Do not pray for tasks equal to your powers.
Pray for powers equal to your tasks.

The Desperate Race

MARY JANE CHAMBERS

I opened the pages of The Washington Post—and stared. A gang of robber-rapists, the paper reported, was prowling the highways close to Washington, D.C., preying on women driving alone at night. The armed thugs would follow their victim on a lonely stretch of road, harassing her until she pulled over and stopped. Dozens of women had been victimized in the past month.

I looked at the story for a long time—but I already knew certain details all too well. My thoughts flashed back to the night two weeks before when I too drove alone—from Alexandria to Mount Vernon, on a five-mile stretch of the George Washington Parkway along the Potomac River.

I had attended a committee meeting at my church in Alexandria until about 9:00 P.M. When I got into my car to go home, out of habit I locked the doors. I was not especially concerned about driving home alone. After all, I'd been married for thirty years, had two grown sons. I'd led a protected life, really. Nobody had ever tried to harm me.

I drove two blocks down Belleview Avenue and swung onto the parkway. My husband and I often drove home from church this way on Sunday morning, when there were picnickers along the roadside and boaters on the Potomac. But now the recreation areas that bordered the road were deserted; there were no streetlights, and in the dark, the parkway, so busy during the day, seemed desolate. *I wish I hadn't come this way*, I thought.

Traffic was light. There were only a few cars in sight, all behind me. I stayed in the right lane while three of them passed me and sped off into the night.

A fourth car pulled up behind me. And stayed there. Apparently its driver was content to follow along at my speed. But the car did seem to be unusually close. I glanced in my rearview mirror, wondering if the driver realized how close he was to me. I guess he didn't.

Then the car drew even closer. Suddenly their headlights flashed, their *bright* lights. I gasped in surprise, quickly tilting up the mirror so I wouldn't be blinded by the glare. But their lights still lit up the interior of my car. Did they have some kind of spotlight?

Now I was worried. I had the strange feeling they were watching me intently. Why were they doing this? Were they kids out on a joyride? Whoever they were, this was a bad joke. And dangerous. "Dear God," I prayed, "make them pass me."

But if anything, they came closer. Bolder and bolder, they were now inches from my back bumper, their lights still trained on my head.

We went a mile, then two. They could see *me* clearly—but I couldn't see them. It seemed to me I'd seen two people in the front seat and another in the back. I wasn't sure. But now it was chillingly clear that these weren't just kids out on a lark. Whoever the dark figures in that car were, they were stalking me. I felt defenseless, and alone.

Near panic, I held tight to the steering wheel as though it could somehow take me out of this danger.

"Please, God," I prayed, "help me to know what to do."

Even before I finished speaking, I felt calmer. I unclenched my fingers and held the steering wheel more lightly. My shoulders relaxed, then my thoughts. And as my panic lessened, a voice sounded firmly in my mind.

Keep going. Don't stop.

But I couldn't stand those lights another minute. If I pulled over, they'd just pass me—wouldn't they? And the ordeal would be over.

You're on a four-lane highway that's practically deserted. They could pass you if they wanted to. Keep moving.

Like a student reviewing a problem in arithmetic, I thought of possible things I could do. I thought about turning off down one of the side roads. Again the inner voice:

You don't know this area very well. You could get lost. Or cornered.

I passed a sign that said, "Speed Limit 45, Radar Enforced."

If I speed up, I thought, *I may be able to attract the attention of the park police.* This time the inner voice was silent. I pressed my foot on the accelerator and saw the speedometer zoom to seventy-five miles an hour.

For a few seconds I was free of the other car, but soon it was back at my bumper again. And no police car—or *any* car—appeared.

I went faster still, pulled ahead a bit, then slowed. So did they. The slower speed was even worse—torture in slow motion.

The feeling of fear took over again. My knuckles were white on the steering wheel. Again I was on the verge of stopping.

Is there something wrong with your car? said the inner voice.

I would have laughed if I hadn't been so frightened. My husband, a car fancier, faithfully kept our car running well.

Are you low on gas?

No, my husband just filled the tank.

Do you have a flat tire?

Obviously not.

This checklist cleared my head. I had no real reason to stop—and if I did I'd be putting myself in the hands of these strangers. I drove on.

Suddenly, to my own surprise, I began to sing. "Amazing Grace," "How Great Thou Art" and other hymns. My pursuers were flooding my car with glaring light. But I could flood it too—with God's strength and love. I sang as loudly as I could.

I was still trembling. But I was determined not to surrender. I began to think of how I could outwit my pursuers.

And you will think of something, the inner voice said. *God is with you.*

I was in familiar territory now, approaching the turnoff to the Mount Vernon highway that would take me to my neighborhood. As the intersection appeared, I pretended I was going to stop at the stop sign. At the last possible moment, I turned the wheel and stepped on the accelerator instead. My car careened around the corner, tires screeching. I raced down the highway like an Indianapolis Speedway driver.

My pursuers were thrown off—but only for a moment. They seemed to be fumbling with their gears, and by the time they recovered, I was almost a block ahead. Out of the reach of their glaring lights.

Again the inner voice spoke before fear could take hold. *Keep moving,* it said. *Don't stop. God is with you.*

Before my pursuers could catch up with me again, another car entered from a side street, inserting itself between us.

I turned off the highway onto Maryland Avenue, heading for home. In my rearview mirror I saw my pursuers turn too. But the other car had slowed them down and given me the lead I needed.

The road curved abruptly to the right—and there, momentarily concealed by the bend, was the entrance to my street! I swerved left again and raced toward my house. When I was barely a block away, I saw my tormentors shoot past behind me on Maryland, pursuing me in the wrong direction. From the way they were speeding, they would be blocks away before realizing they had lost me.

After following me down three different roads, they had missed the last turn! As I shut and locked the door of my home behind me, I almost cried with relief. Our house is on a cul-de-sac. If they hadn't missed that last turn they might have trapped me.

Now, two weeks later, as I looked at the newspaper account about these criminals, I felt horror—and yet a feeling of strength as well. "Aren't you terrified to go out at night now?" a friend had asked when I told her my story.

I'm definitely more cautious now. I always take sensible precautions when driving alone, especially after dark. But I'm not cowering in my house, living the life of a timid recluse. Fear didn't cause me to panic and pull over that night—and it's not going to stop me now.

I may drive down another dark road where terror and desperation await. Or I may find myself faced with some other emergency that seems hopeless. I know now that my hope and security reside in God, who guides me down every road and through every crisis.

Whatever comes, I will never have to face it alone.

Definition

AUTHOR UNKNOWN

> Courage:
> Fear that has said its prayers.

A Story of Answered Prayer

BRIG. GEN. AND MRS. JAMES L. DOZIER

GENERAL JAMES L. DOZIER: My wife and I glance at each other.

Our apartment doorbell just rang; someone is outside in the hall. This is strange; visitors usually first ring the building-entrance bell downstairs.

As deputy chief of staff for logistics in a headquarters in the North Atlantic Treaty Organization's Southern Region, I have just returned from work to our apartment here in Verona, Italy. It is 5:30 P.M., December 17, 1981, and Judy is preparing dinner.

She touches my arm as I step toward the door. "I don't like it when the doorbell rings on our level," she says.

"I'm sure it's all right," I say, "probably one of the building people."

As I open the door it appears I'm right. Two bearded men in dark clothing politely explain they are plumbers. The smaller one carries a tool bag. Water, they say, is dripping into the apartment below and they need to find out if any of our fixtures is leaking.

I take them down the hall to the utility room where they seem to find everything in order. The bigger man uses an Italian word I don't understand so I go back to the kitchen and pick up my Italian-English dictionary. I'm suddenly jumped from the rear by one of the men.

Judy gasps as the other grabs her and we look into the muzzles of two pistols.

"We are the Red Brigades!" barks one of the men. The Red Brigades. The infamous terrorist group in Italy who have kid-napped and murdered numerous government and business leaders.

The smaller man pushes Judy to the floor while the large one and I continue to struggle. I fight, but pain explodes in my head from a blow and I crumple. I see Judy on her knees with a pistol pointed at her head and I stop fighting.

My arms are jerked behind me, steel handcuffs clamp my wrists; a gag is jammed into my jaws, and a cloth blinds me. Helpless, I hear the men let others into the apartment. Desk and bureau drawers clatter open and papers rustle as they ransack. I know they won't find anything confidential. But I worry about Judy and pray she won't be harmed.

Something sounding hollow and heavy is dragged up to me. Hands grasp me and I am stuffed into a large trunk.

I remember Aldo Moro, Italy's former prime minister, who was found dead in a car trunk fifty-four days after his kidnapping by the Red Brigades. The box lurches as I'm carried downstairs, and then it is slid onto a hard surface. A truck engine roars and we bounce over streets.

My chest begins to pound and I take small breaths to conserve oxygen. From time to time the lid flies back and cool fresh air pours in. Hands check my pulse; then the lid slams shut. They want to keep me alive, for the moment anyway. We rumble on and the trunk I'm in is transferred to what seems to be a car. Finally, we stop, and my trunk is lugged into a building. An elevator motor whines; controls click and buzz as we rise, drop and ascend. They are trying to disorient me. The door clangs open, I'm carried a short distance. The lid lifts; I am pulled out and lugged through what seems to be a small opening and dropped onto a cot. The gag and blindfold are removed and I sit blinking.

I'm inside a blue canvas cubicle about six feet square; it seems to be part of a tent erected inside an apartment. Three masked men chain my right wrist and left ankle to the metal cot. There is just enough slack in the shackles to reach a chemical toilet in a corner. This is my prison. For how long?

MRS. JAMES L. DOZIER: I lie face down on the floor, ankles chained to wrists. I feel strangely calm. God must give this inner strength when we need it most. Just before the big man blindfolds me, I see a trunk by our kitchen door. I sense it is for Jim. Will I ever see him again? I pray for guidance to know when it will be safe to call for help.

A terrorist drags me down the hall to a room. I remain motionless while praying for Jim. Finally, the men leave. I dislodge the blindfold and look up into the blue flame of the water heater in our bathroom. Still chained wrist to ankle, I hunch along the tiles to the washing machine. I bang its metal side with my knees and call for help. But I do not know that our neighbors in the apartment below sit in the other end of their flat watching television. No one hears me.

Three hours have passed since Jim was taken. My knee is numb from thumping the washer, and my voice is dwindling to a croak. The doorbell rings; I call out again. Minutes later the glass crashes in a terrace window and the man who lives below rushes in crying, "*O mio Dio!*" Already his wife has phoned the police. Our neighbor's daughter had heard my calls when she had gone to the bathroom, which lies just below ours.

GEN. D.: Is Judy safe? It's all I can think of. My captors assure me that she is, and I sink back on the cot breathing thanks. I am not afraid of death; it has been a close companion for years, especially during combat. I know that death is only a transition into another life, a much better one promised by our Lord. But I am concerned for my family; we have a grown son and daughter and I don't want them to worry. I pray for them and everyone involved in this, that we maintain our proper perspective and be sensitive to God's guidance.

I survey my cell. In the outer section of the tent a masked guard sits, a call button taped to his chair arm. Another guard steps in and slips a stereo headset on my head. It is to prevent me from overhearing conversations. I am stunned by the high, piercing volume of hard rock music.

The din of shrieking crescendoes and exploding drums is excruciating. I have never cared for rock and roll and slump back onto the cot; the steel chains numb my wrist and ankle. How much longer can I stand this? I reach for the earphones but my guard is half out of his chair, sternly shaking his head no. Finally my mind turns off the noise.

The net. I gotta stay in the net.

Staying in the net is Army parlance for keeping in radio communication with your commander and fellow troops while out in the field. It is vital during battle; once you are out of the net, you are in trouble. My net with my Commander is maintained through prayer. Now more than ever I must keep in communication with my Commander. I learned this, long before my Army days, back in Arcadia, Florida. Dad died when I was fourteen, and Mom supported my sister and me there by teaching school. Only five feet tall, she was a spiritual powerhouse, continuing her teaching Sundays at the Methodist church. It was she who taught me to stay in the net. "God created you for a purpose, Jim," she said, "and the way to fulfill it is to keep in close touch with Him."

Keep in touch with Him. I set my mind on this. I see no human faces, only black masks. No matter what happens I know He will guide me and this whole affair will work out for the best. His will shall be done. A deep peace floods me and I fall asleep.

I awaken. They bring me toast and milk for breakfast. Now my inquisition begins. A terrorist squatting on the floor fires questions about NATO, my political beliefs.

I feel vulnerable. I do not want to discredit my country, Italy or NATO, and I pray for guidance. Then I feel a strange calm, as if I am in the company of others, other people who are praying for me, guiding me. *I'm trying hard to stay in the net.*

I answer the questions with harmless information. When we finish, they return my earphones. I ask for different music. One brings George Gershwin's *Rhapsody in Blue*. I sigh gratefully, but the volume is still high and my hearing is deteriorating.

I cannot tell time, either, as they took my watch. However, I find that when my guard is reading a magazine or talking with someone I can sneak the headset away from my ears an inch or so and hear sounds outside the building.

There are street noises, and I soon make out the typical traffic pattern of an Italian city. First, the morning rush hour, then the early afternoon *reposo*, with traffic picking up about 5:00 P.M., until the stores close at eight or so, and everything dropping off at midnight.

Now I can track passing days, and I attempt to follow a daily regimen, beginning and ending each day with push-ups, sit-ups and other exercises. I ask for a Bible and other books; they bring me only novels and news magazines. Perhaps they don't have an English Bible handy. I am grateful that I have read it through and remember some of it.

MRS. D. The Red Brigades have issued their first communique. It had been deposited in a trash container in Rome. They call Jim a "NATO hangman" and say that he has been taken to a "people's prison and will be submitted to proletarian justice." They say they have declared war on the entire NATO alliance as a "structure of military occupation."

Their fuzzy snapshot shows a bruise under Jim's left eye. The police assure me that a massive search is on. All that can possibly be done is being done.

Even in my sleep I think of Jim. My dream last night was so vivid. It was as if we were talking. The strange thing about it was Jim's hair; instead of his usual crew cut, it was long and wavy. I know God sometimes speaks to us through dreams. Is there some meaning in this? I don't know and continue to pray for him.

GEN. D. I feel a closeness with Judy as if she were with me. I *know* she is praying for me; I sense it. After twenty-six years of marriage there is a special relationship that distance and prisons cannot touch.

A week has passed since our separation and my face itches from beard growth. The earphones' volume has been lowered, but I'm tired of Gershwin. I have yet to see a human face, only photos in old copies of *Time* and *Newsweek* that my masked captors bring. They clip out the stories they don't want me to see, but they did give me a news photo of Judy; it becomes my pinup picture.

I pray for her peace of mind, for she knows my captors' reputation for cold-blooded murder. In spite of my predicament, I remain optimistic about the outcome. I am helped by something quite strong, a force supporting me like the lift one feels from an ocean wave, a powerful buoyancy.

I had the first feeling of this wave several days ago while I was doing pushups; a vivid impression came to me of my executive officer. He is a deep-thinking friend. I've always felt confident about bouncing my thoughts off of him. At first I wondered why I felt his presence so closely; then I knew. He was praying for me. I felt invigorated.

A few days later, while I was playing solitaire, I sensed the closeness of another friend. He teaches in the American school in Verona and is a gentle man who truly lives his faith.

It happened again yesterday afternoon; this time it was an American missionary who ministers to American servicemen in Vicenza. I know now he is ministering to me.

And this morning while reading I found myself chuckling; it wasn't the book but a graphic impression of the feisty wife of a fellow general officer. She is an outspoken woman, and I can just imagine her calling Judy and saying, "Golly, as soon as I leave, things go to h--- in a hand-basket." She had left Europe shortly before I was kidnapped.

Now I know that not only Judy but all our friends—and other people—are praying for me. I know that all the resources of my country and Italy are at work endeavoring to free me. But nothing is more powerful than prayer. I long to thank these people who are praying for me, and I do so, in prayer.

MRS. D. Here in Verona, where my daughter and son have come to spend Christmas, the postmen bring packets of mail from Italians who write that they are praying for Jim. We also pick up more mail from Americans at our post office. They write of prayer chains and groups meeting on Jim's behalf.

It seems that prayers are rising for Jim around the clock every-where. And friends are so supportive. The American and Italian communities have been such a help, and prayer groups are being organized worldwide.

The momentum appears to be building. I find myself smiling for the first time in weeks. What would we do without caring friends? I am also deeply touched by the many Italians who bashfully come to our door with flowers and gifts. So many say they are praying to Saint Anthony. "He is the one who finds anything missing," an elderly woman assures me. "I pray for him to find your husband. He will; you wait, you see."

It is Christmas Eve, 1981. As we return from chapel, I see the little candle in our window. It burns every night. It was a gift from a local mother whose little boy insisted that she buy it for "the general." As I light it, I am reminded of the prayers and love of people everywhere.

GEN. D. From my reckoning I believe Christmas has passed. But my guards, who seem to know everything, told me about our son's and daughter's and my sister's arrival in Verona. I'm grateful for that, but these chains are a nuisance. My unwashed body smells.

MRS. D. Jim has been reported dead. An anonymous caller told the police that he had been killed and hinted where his body could be found. The authorities are dragging a lake in the mountains. Can I keep my thoughts on God with such horrible news? But isn't this what Jim used to call "staying in the net"?

GEN. D. The hoaxes I read about in news magazines regarding my death disturb me and I complain to my captors. They snort and say they "do not do tricks like that." I believe them. They play for keeps. But the waiting is tedious. A month has gone by; my beard is full and my hair long and wavy, not like the crew cut I have had all my life. But the chains . . . the chains are a nuisance. Wasn't there something in the Bible about Peter being in chains? I can't exactly remember. If Mom were here she'd know. Even after I graduated from West Point in 1956 and married Judy, Mom continued to send us copies of her weekly Sunday school lessons.

I smile in memory. When she was nearly sixty, she gave God what she called "an extra mile" by spending a year in India as a missionary. I lean back on the cot, my eyes moistening. Mom died just a year and a half ago but I can sense her presence. If she could do what she did, then I should be able to do whatever God expects of me right here, chains and all.

MRS. D. Six weeks have passed and the news isn't good. The authorities assure me that thousands of special investigators are searching for Jim. Yet to the press they express total frustration. "Dozier," said one top official, "could well be in the hands of the Martians, for all we know." Worse, the Red Brigades won't discuss Jim's release. "Negotiate? For what?" demands their latest communique. "The proletariat has nothing to negotiate with the bourgeoisie."

I have left Verona, first to visit friends in Naples and then on to Germany to stay with other close friends. I awaken this January morning feeling very optimistic. Why? I walk into the bathroom and look into the mirror wondering. All I know is that this is the day that the Lord has made and I should rejoice and be glad in it. But even when your husband has been a prisoner for forty-two days?

GEN. D. I am starting to read the novel 1984 by George Orwell. It is not the most enjoyable story to read when a captive. "Big Brother" is all-pervasive. Yet I only have to remember the most powerful force of all, the love of our Father against whom the principalities and evils of this world are nothing.

My calculations tell me that I'm somewhere around my fortieth day of captivity. Jesus spent forty days alone in the desert. I guess we all have to wander through our own wilderness at some time or another. Yet, something strange has been happening. Lately, I have found myself playing a scenario in my mind over and over of what I will face on my release or rescue: the press conferences, debriefings. From where do such thoughts come?

There is a crash of splintering wood outside my tent, scuffling and shouts. My guard leaps to his feet and, with pistol aimed generally toward me, looks out the tent flap. A masked man bursts in and with one blow crumples him unconscious. Is it a rival gang invasion? My chains clattering, I grasp the masked invader, then feel the bulletproof vest under his black sweater. He hugs me and laughs. He is a commando from Italy's crack anti-terrorist unit. The locks on my two chains are released and they fall away; and I am escorted downstairs to a waiting car. They tell me that six thousand Italian investigators, working closely with the American and European experts, had conducted a mammoth sweep of suspects, following thousands of clues that led them to this apartment building in Padua, a town forty-eight miles east of Verona.

Thank God it is over.

MRS. D. I tell my friends how great I feel. We continue with our plans, and while preparing lunch, phone calls start to come in. Jim has been rescued! He's in good health and waiting for me in

Italy. As our friends encircle me, cheering and crying, I stand in stunned silence. Our prayers have been answered—Jim is safe and coming home!

They say that Jim had been found in Padua. As with all Italian cities, it has a patron saint. The patron saint of Padua is Saint Anthony.

GEN. D. Strange how the impressions given me in captivity have worked out in reality—the press conferences, the welcomes by the authorities and friends.

But, above all, one salient truth has been proven to me in a most amazing way. That our prayers for others, expressed in the love of God, can be our most powerful communication with them, transcending time and space.

For when I sat down with my executive officer, the American schoolteacher, the fellow general officer's wife, the American missionary and the many others whose loving, sustaining presences came to me in captivity so vividly, I learned in comparing notes with them that these happened at the very time they were earnestly praying for me.

"Who shall separate us from the love of Christ?" asks the Apostle Paul (Romans 8:35, 37). "Shall tribulation, or distress, or persecution, or famine, or nakedness, or peril, or sword?"

"Nay," is his ringing answer, for "in all these things we are more than conquerors through him that loved us!"

The Reasons Why

AUTHOR UNKNOWN

> Not till the loom is silent,
> And the shuttles cease to fly,
> Shall God unfold the canvas,
> And reveal the reasons why
> The dark threads are as needful
> In the Weaver's skillful hand
> As the threads of gold and silver
> In the pattern He has planned.

12.

Prayer That Heals

At Even, When the Sun Was Set

At even, when the sun was set,
  The sick, O Lord, around Thee lay;
O in what divers pains they met!
  O with what joy they went away!

Once more 'tis eventide, and we,
  Oppressed with various ills draw near;
What if Thy form we cannot see,
  We know and feel that Thou art here.

O Saviour Christ, our woes dispel:
  For some are sick, and some are sad,
And some have never loved Thee well,
  And some have lost the love they had;

. . .

Thy touch has still its ancient power;
  No word from Thee can fruitless fall:
Hear in this solemn evening hour,
  And in Thy mercy heal us all.

HENRY TWELLS
(1823–1900)

A Different Kind of Healing

VICTOR HERBERT

Guillain-Barré Syndrome is a rare and mysterious nerve illness named for the two French physicians who identified it. At its onset the patient feels a numbness in the muscles, followed by a paralysis that can advance rapidly through the body. If the lungs become totally disabled, the victim suffocates.

In 1962 I had a mild case of Guillain-Barré Syndrome. When I was back on my feet, the doctor warned me that it could recur. I was a busy young man with a wife, four kids and a great job as a sales engineer; it was easy to put that brush with GBS behind me. In fact, I forgot about it for two decades. Then came a summer morning in 1982 when I was a not-so-young-man of fifty-four.

I awakened to a strange tingling in the fingers of both hands. Like pins and needles. Then, as I swung my legs off the bed, I noticed that my thighs felt heavy. When I tried to stand, my knees buckled. I fell to the bed. I knew I'd felt that awful weakness once before.

By the time I was hospitalized that Friday afternoon, the weakness in my legs had become numbness. The next day, my belly and bowels became useless. My wife, Shirley, spent Saturday night in a chair in my room because I was unable to move from the waist down and felt the numbness moving up my chest. I was paralyzed.

On Sunday morning, while Shirley was at home changing clothes, the numbness started creeping into my lungs and throat. I was scared. I felt alone and helpless. In the dim, quiet hospital room I lay motionless, feeling something I had never felt before. A calling out from deep inside myself. A need that was as strong and real as hunger. I wanted God. I craved Him.

Years before, I'd left my faith behind when I left home for college. Science, I'd thought then, was a more reasonable source of answers to life than religion. Now, with my lungs turning to stone, I longed for God. Not only for the comfort of believing in Him. Even more, I wanted to feel I could entrust Shirley to His care. I needed to talk to Him about her.

As a child in a churchgoing family, I'd learned the Lord's Prayer. Now, groping for the old half-remembered phrases, I began to say it aloud. Though my voice was thin and rusty, the words sounded good to my ears. At the end I asked, "Please, Lord, take care of Shirley when I go."

Moments later I was gasping for breath. When I came to, I was in the Intensive Care Unit. Only my mind seemed to be functioning. It told me that I was as far removed from normal human life as a man could get. My body felt mummified. I was paralyzed from the chin down, bristling with plastic tubes that took care of my physical needs and dripped medicine into my veins. A respirator did my breathing for me. I couldn't move a muscle except for my eyelids. My field of vision was limited to a patch of ceiling and my communication consisted of spelling out words by blinking my eyes when someone pointed to letters on an alphabet card.

For two weeks the doctors worked on me, using an experimental treatment that involved exchanging my blood plasma for saline. Then the worst possible thing happened. I got pneumonia. And lost my last shred of humanity. My mind.

It happened this way. Hoping to protect me from further lung infection and from blood clots, the medical team decided to put me in a motorized bed that would keep my body in motion artificially. A Stryker frame, it was called. My body was held in place by a special covering to keep me from falling off as it turned me from side-to-side twenty-four hours a day, never stopping. It was like being lashed to the wing of an airplane that was banking steeply in a turn, first one way and then the other.

Very soon, my eyes began playing tricks on me. During the constant bizarre tipping and turning, my narrowed vision caught strange shadows. In the dim lights of the ICU, the tubes, bags and machinery took on eerie shapes. Shapes that moved menacingly. Shapes that became mad dogs, a pack of them milling viciously beneath my bed, snapping as my foot and hand dipped only inches from the floor, into their midst.

I was hallucinating, and I couldn't even cry out for help! Though I had been sending thought-prayers to God ever since my first awkward "Lord's Prayer," I now lost my mental grip on Him. Paranoia set in. The shadows of the men and women who tended my machines were those of torturers who were trying to kill me and make it look like an accident. I even spelled out M-U-R-D-E-R on the alphabet card with eye-blinks when Shirley held it up.

One day my family and the doctors and nurses spent hours convincing me that delirium from the pneumonia (which had collapsed one lung), lack of rest and my isolation were the problem. I believed them in the light of day, but that night, as shadows flickered on the walls and the "airplane" banked with me strapped to the wing, I slipped into delusion again. Into terror. *Lord,* I cried out in my mind, *keep me out of this hell. Please God! Show me how to stay with You.*

Briefly my bed twisted into a level position. A woman came into my sight line. A woman with reddish-gold hair and the saddest look on her face. I saw her only for a moment, and then the bed tilted away, down toward the other side, where the ugly shadows waited. Fiercely, I made myself concentrate on her to ward off the nightmare. I knew *she* was real because I'd glimpsed that reddish-gold hair in the daytime. She was the mother of a sixteen-year-old boy who'd been in the next cubicle—and he wasn't expected to live, according to the low whispers of his relatives.

I had never seen the boy, but his mother's face stayed in my mind. A face anguished with despair for her son's life. I knew despair. I'd felt it for my own life on the first Sunday here. Suddenly I wanted to comfort that mother. But what in the world could I do? Paralyzed, down with pneumonia, pinned to a weird revolving bed, no voice, half out of my mind . . .

I can't even help myself, I thought. *Only I did* drag *myself out of despair that Sunday . . . when I prayed.*

At that moment I said another prayer. Involuntarily, in a rush of compassion.

O Lord, remember me? A sad, sad woman is here. Her son is nearly dead. She's so scared. She held that boy in her arms as a tiny baby fresh from You and as a little boy afraid in the dark, and she wants to see him grow up. She's thinking of all the little moments that mounted up to all this love she feels. Please, Lord, keep her in Your loving care. Ease her mind. Wrap that boy in Your healing Spirit. Save him, Lord. I love him, too. I love her. . . .

An hour later, concentrating on prayer for the mother and son, I was surprised to see that what had once been a monstrous alligator was no more than my wastebasket with a jagged package protruding from it. My panic was gone.

Night and day I prayed—and the hallucinations stayed at bay. Gradually, the whispers of the boy's relatives were less gloomy, and hope flickered in his mother's eyes. Then the doctor said he *would* recover. I was still praying for this boy I couldn't see, whose life had become infinitely precious to me, when a new patient came into the bed on the other side of me.

I could see the new occupant because his bed was hoisted high at an angle. All but his face was in a cast or bandaged. A motorcycle policeman, he'd been hit by a car while on duty. Immediately I began to pray for him, too. A wondrous feeling of strength swept through me with each prayer, as I concentrated on his bandaged limbs, one after another. Before long, the glow of God's healing seemed to spread over me and the equipment between our beds, and to pour right into the swathed figure. In time the policeman left the ICU, and eventually I learned that he was back on duty.

More time passed and I, too, left the Intensive Care Unit. And I recovered from Guillain-Barré Syndrome—a gift from God and a dedicated medical staff. Later I came across a Bible passage that summed up my experience and pointed the way to the future. "Keep sane and sober for your prayers. Above all hold unfailing your love for one another, since love covers a multitude of sins. Practice hospitality ungrudgingly to one another. As each has received a gift, employ it for one another" (1 Peter 4:7–10, RSV).

I believe that I kept sane *because* of my prayers for others. I had no idea that in helping them I'd be helping myself. I'll never forget that when I asked God to release me from my personal hell, He pointed me to the face of another human being.

How Does God Heal?

MICHELE STEGMAN

For many years my Grandmother Adams suffered from an excruciating pain in her jaw, and the doctors couldn't seem to help her. Grandmother lived in the Kentucky hills. She was a woman of strong faith, yet she did not pray for her healing.

Often she'd told me stories of how people, including my grandfather, had been cured by faith healers. One day when her pain seemed particularly intense, I said, "Didn't you tell me that James Wright can heal pains?"

"Yes," she nodded.

"Then go to him," I pressed.

"Oh, I'll see him at church sometime," she said in a tone that told me she would not.

Then it occurred to me that I had chided Grandmother for not praying for herself, yet never once had *I* prayed for her! Right then and there I began to ask God to heal her.

A few weeks later Grandmother found another doctor who thought he could help. She entered the hospital, received treatment and was cured. Her pain was gone.

Now I was disturbed again. *Well,* I thought, *faith and prayer hadn't healed Grandmother after all. The doctor had. God did not answer my prayer.*

Or had He?

Pals

PATRICIA BRADY

Although the McCurdy family lives around the corner from us, my son Jackie didn't really get to know Danny McCurdy until they started school. I guess it was my fault. Even though I truly like people, it's difficult for me to be the one who reaches out first. I'm always afraid I'll seem a little foolish.

Once Jackie and Danny did get acquainted, though, it became apparent to me that the bond of love between them was something special. I'd never seen anything like it in the friendships of my three older children. And I wasn't the only one who thought the boys' closeness rare. As the two little pals became a familiar sight in our neighborhood, more than one neighbor commented, "I never see those boys argue." And it was true. Whatever activity one suggested, the other agreed to.

Because of their physical appearances, it was easy to spot them at play. Jackie's blue eyes and blond hair contrasted sharply with Danny's brown eyes and straight dark hair. Unfortunately, there was a greater—though invisible—contrast between them. Jackie's excellent health was marred only by eczema on his legs, but Danny had lost a kidney to cancer before he started kindergarten.

When the boys turned seven, Danny's cancer recurred. This

time part of his right lung was removed, and chemotherapy treatments were started. The treatments made Danny violently ill, and whenever I heard he was having a bad day, I had only to look at Jackie to confirm it. Jackie, who visited Danny whenever possible, would get so uptight he couldn't sit still, and he would scratch at his eczema more than ever.

Soon the chemotherapy caused all of Danny's hair to fall out. He tried to conceal his head by covering it with a red Phillies baseball cap. Whether Danny was sitting in class or at our supper table, the bright red cap clung to his head.

At first, I didn't realize why Jackie was badgering me for a cap exactly like Danny's. But as soon as he got it, Jackie placed the cap on his head the same way Danny wore it—with the brim turned toward the back. And, like Danny's, Jackie's cap stayed firmly in place from sunup to sundown. No amount of persuasion could convince him to take it off.

That July there was a special healing service at our parish church, and I had a growing feeling that Danny should attend it. There were to be several priests on hand to anoint the sick with oil. I asked Lorraine McCurdy, Danny's mother, if my husband Jack and I could take Danny. She agreed to let him go.

When the evening of the mass arrived, Jack and I took our children and Danny to the church. It was hot and crowded inside. Perspiration began to darken the rims of the two red baseball caps and trickle down the boys' faces, but neither removed his cap.

Finally it was time for those seeking healing to go to the altar. "How about it, Danny?" I asked. "Do you want to go up and ask the Lord for a healing?"

"Nah," Danny said, his lashless brown eyes avoiding those of the people rising from their seats. "I'm sick and tired of being prayed over."

I knew, of course, that it was actually a case of "sick and tired of being stared at," something Danny had come to dread. Even though I understood that feeling only too well, I was upset by his answer. If anybody in that church needed a healing, it was Danny.

"What are we going to do?" I whispered frantically to Jack.

"I've got an idea that might work," Jack answered softly. Turning to Jackie, he said, "What about you, Jackie? Would you like to have prayers for your rash?"

I don't know what went through Jackie's mind as he pondered his father's question, but I know what raced through mine. *Do it for Danny, Jackie,* I pleaded silently. *Do it for Danny.*

"Okay," Jackie decided. "I'll get my rash prayed over."

My husband and I stood up and started to move forward. Our son slid from his seat and headed for the end of one of the lines. Danny, tugging at his cap, followed at his heels.

When we finally inched our way to the altar, we found that we'd been waiting in Father Curran's line. He was our parish priest and knew the boys' needs even better than they themselves did.

"Well, Jackie," he said. "What healing do you want from the Lord?"

"I want to get rid of this itchy rash, Father," he said, pointing to his bare legs.

Then Father Curran looked at Danny and his gaze softened. "And what about you, Danny? What do you want?"

Danny grinned shyly. "I'm not here for me, Father. I'm here for Jackie's rash."

Father Curran anointed the boys with oil and, placing a hand on each, began to pray. Jack and I, who were standing behind them, also laid our hands upon the children and prayed along with Father Curran. Jackie's rash practically forgotten, we silently begged God for Danny's life.

A few days later I was sitting on the beach at the lake, watching the two red caps bobbing about in the water. Jenny, a friend from church, joined me.

"Pat," she said joyously, "Danny's been healed."

My heart leaped. "How do you know?"

"I had a vision of Danny dashing into the lake. And you know what? He wasn't wearing his baseball cap. His hair had grown back in thick, black curls."

I wanted desperately to share Jenny's confidence, but something was wrong with that vision. Danny's hair had been straight. Yet soon after that, Lorraine McCurdy told me she could see hair starting to appear on Danny's scalp. And when it was finally in, we could all see for ourselves that it was thick—and curly.

When Danny returned to the hospital for his checkup, the doctors informed the McCurdys that Danny had responded to treatment. The cancer was arrested. The rejoicing in the Lord that took place in our parish was indescribable. In fact, my own gratitude to God was so overwhelming that weeks passed before I realized Jackie wasn't scratching at his eczema.

"Come here, Jackie," I said the afternoon it finally occurred to me. "Let me see your legs." He rolled up his jeans. The skin on his legs was clear.

Four years have passed* since the night of the healing service. Danny and Jackie, now eleven, are as close as ever and—except that Danny's hair has returned to its naturally straight state—are pretty much the same as the summer they were healed.

As if those of us who witnessed this miracle from God weren't blessed enough, He has heaped upon us His grace to overflowing. For no matter what the future holds for Danny and Jackie, the Lord has spoken to all of us through the love of two small boys. Hasn't he shown us firsthand how to become like children so that we, too, may enter the kingdom of Heaven?

As for me, I got a healing of my own. Now, whenever I find myself in a situation where I feel a little foolish reaching out, all I have to do is think back to the night of the healing mass and that desperately ill little boy who did not hesitate to step forward—no matter how "foolish" he may have felt—to help his friend.

Can I do less?

Healing The Hurt In Your Heart

VIRGINIA LIVELY

The woman kneeling at the altar rail was in pain—all of us taking part in the healing service could see that. Her face showed her intense agony.

"Migraine," the minister whispered to me as we moved toward her down the line of kneeling people.

Then I was standing in front of her. "I have migraine headaches," she explained. I laid my hands on her head and asked Jesus who loved her to take this pain away. Her mouth relaxed, and she opened her eyes like someone waked from a bad dream.

"It's gone!" she whispered.

---

*Written in 1982.

"Thank You, Lord!" said the minister. "Thank You!" the congregation echoed. "Thank You!" I repeated, most awestruck of all.

Although it was nine years since God had called me to His ministry of healing, I still could never get over the joyous surprise of it. My chief surprise was that He could use me—a middle-aged housewife with a spreading waistline and a kitchen in need of new linoleum—to reach out to people who hurt. But because it happened, over and over again, I'd stopped trying to figure it out and simply and gratefully gone ahead.

Why, then, as this now smiling woman went back to her pew, was I gripped with a strange uneasiness? A person had been in pain. The pain was gone. But all through the minister's closing prayers, I was puzzled.

Then I remembered something which was to shed light for me on the whole mystery of healing. I remembered that I had seen this lady before. It was right here in this same little Episcopal church the last time I'd been here, three years before. She had come forward with a blinding headache that night too. And God had healed her.

Then why was she back tonight? Was God's healing only temporary? Did it wear out and need renewing from time to time—like kitchen linoleum? Or was there something in this lady's life deeper than the migraine that needed healing? Something that lay behind the headaches and made them happen, something that she had never brought to the altar rail?

As people started up the aisle, I got to the woman's side and asked if she could stay behind. And so in a quiet pew we talked. When, I asked, had this last attack begun?

She thought a moment. "I guess it was just after Jeannie was so upset. She's our youngest, and you know how kids are. The older ones wouldn't let her into their clubhouse."

The more we talked, the more we saw a pattern. The headaches seemed to begin when she saw a child mistreated. A story in the paper, a church appeal for hungry orphans, one of her own youngsters up against life's small injustices, any of these could trigger an incapacitating attack that might send her to bed for days. And yet her own childhood, she said, had been unusually happy.

"My stepfather was a wonderful man. You see, mom wasn't married when she had me. But then she married my stepfather, and he raised me just like one of his own. We were a very religious family. Dad was superintendent of the Sunday school, and mom did the flowers, and I sang in the choir, funny as it seems."

"Why funny?"

"Because I—" The woman's eyes grew huge. "Because I can never go to heaven!"

She sat blinking in the dim-lit sanctuary. "I remember my stepfather saying it! He said he loved me and he'd give me everything he could here on earth but little girls like me could never go to heaven."

She had not thought of it with the conscious mind, perhaps, but beneath all the other thoughts of her life had lain this monstrous image of an unjust God.

Before we left the church that night, we went to the altar rail, just she and I, and held up to God this ugly, twisted picture of Himself. "Take it away, Father," I asked, "and show her Jesus instead." This is one reason why Jesus came, I told her, so we can know what God is really like. "Read the Gospels," I suggested. "Read them over and over until you have such a firsthand knowledge of Him."

That night, I know from subsequent letters, was the beginning of real healing for this woman. But it also marked a change in my own life. From that evening on, as people described the aches and pains which led them to seek God's divine healing power, I began listening for the deeper aches.

And I made an astonishing discovery. When we got down to the underlying problem, time after time, it was not medical, nor even, at its deepest, psychological. The real trouble was spiritual. And it was precisely the same problem—in a thousand forms—that the woman with the migraines had. These people had trouble loving God.

Some experience, some early training, some false concept, stood between them and true trust.

And there was the businessman who, deep down, did not want to be healed of his alcoholism. The drinking bouts, we began to notice, would start just when he was on the verge of some big sale or about to meet a potential customer. It turned out that he was the son of a pious but unsuccessful shoe salesman who had made a virtue of failure and taught that wealth is contrary to the will of God. My friend couldn't face success. He was afraid of his heavenly Father and didn't want to hurt his earthly father.

The more important a person's faith is to him, the more successfully he has usually hidden from himself this deep distrust of God. People will talk to me almost eagerly about the most agonizing physical condition or the saddest family relationship, but are tongue-tied when it comes to implicating God in these things.

I remember a minister who came to the house relating experiences of strangling attacks of asthma. His story was a familiar one of terror-filled nights and painful days.

When he had finished, I did not immediately begin to pray for healing as I once would have done. Instead I asked him to tell me about his very first asthma attack, and I prayed silently that Jesus would help him expose the real problem.

There was a long, long silence. Then haltingly he began to recall a hunting trip he had missed as a teenager. He was to have left in the morning with a friend and the friend's father, when he had waked in the night struggling for breath. "I wanted to go especially badly because I had no father of my own. You see, when I was nine my own father—my father—" And then this gray-haired man burst into tears. I have discovered that when the root problem is touched at last, there is usually anger or tears or both.

Chokingly the story came out. A well-meaning friend, trying to ease a little boy's grief, had explained to him that God had taken his father because He loved him and wanted him in heaven. And the little boy who loved and wanted his father too had grown up with an unacknowledged fury at a selfish God.

But now that the painful truth was out, we could pray for genuine healing, not just of the asthma but of the far deeper constriction at the very source of this man's life and health.

A portion of the prayer we offered together, which brought about the healing of that childhood memory of caprice and cruelty, may help others put to rest the deep hurts, fears and misunderstandings that trouble most of us.

"Jesus, we know that You are perfect love. But we confess that there are blind spots in our souls that hide this love from us. We ask for Your light in these dark places now, although we know that light can be painful. Burn away any false old images we have built and show us Yourself. Amen."

Immortal Love

JOHN GREENLEAF WHITTIER (1807–1892)

Immortal Love, forever full,
  Forever flowing free,
Forever shared, forever whole,
  A never-ebbing sea!

We may not climb the heavenly steeps
  To bring the Lord Christ down;
In vain we search the lowest deeps,
  For Him no depths can drown.

But warm, sweet, tender, even yet
  A present help is He;
And faith has still its Olivet
  And love its Galilee.

The healing of His seamless dress
  Is by our beds of pain;
We touch Him in life's throng and press,
  And we are whole again.

13.

Unexpected Answers

The Good No

So often our self-centered prayers,
If granted, could bring only woe.
How glad we should be that God cares,
And loves us enough to say, "No."

MARY HAMLETT GOODMAN

When Your Prayers Seem Unanswered

CONSTANCE FOSTER

What are we to conclude when we have prayed for a long time and nothing seems to be any different from before? Is God whimsical, given to listening to one person but turning a deaf ear on another, or hearing us on some occasions and ignoring us on others? Many people ask themselves these questions. When they pray and things remain much the same or even grow worse, they may come to the conclusion that prayer is at best uncertain and at worst futile.

I became so much interested in this subject of apparently unanswered prayer that for several years now I have been gathering records of such instances.

Carol W. was a young college student when she first came to my attention. In spite of hard work and great ambition, Carol was failing to make passing grades in certain subjects and had been warned that unless she did well on her term examinations, she would be dropped at the end of the year. Carol was praying sincerely for success in her exams. But a month later she phoned me and her first words were, "Well, I prayed but nothing happened."

Carol had flunked two courses and the college dropped her. Certainly surface appearances here would seem to justify her conclusion that "nothing happened" as the result of prayer. But wait! And never forget that God knows more than we do about what is for our highest good.

A few weeks after she returned home, Carol consulted a psychologist who was an expert at determining in what areas an individual's best talents lay. He gave her a battery of aptitude tests that revealed she was extremely gifted in spatial perception and mechanical ability. They also showed that she was not naturally a good student where abstract subjects, such as she had taken at college, were concerned.

Carol took a course at a technical school in X-ray therapy and medical techniques. Today she is head of a large hospital laboratory with a dozen assistants under her direction, making a splendid salary and happy in her work. Did nothing happen when she prayed? Graduation from a liberal arts college was not the right answer to her needs and abilities. Carol didn't know it. But God did.

Now let us turn to another example of apparently unanswered prayer. It concerns an elderly widow whose husband's death had left her almost destitute and in danger of losing her large home. She could no longer meet the heavy expense of maintaining it. Mrs. Horton wrote me for prayers that she might be able by some miracle to keep it, together with all her cherished possessions. A few months later another letter from her reached me. "We both prayed," she wrote, "but nothing happened." The house was to be sold at auction the following week. Mrs. Horton was heartbroken.

During the next few days Mrs. Horton went through her house with tear-stained eyes, sorting and discarding the accumulation of long years of living in it. In the attic she ran across an old stamp collection that had been in her husband's family for years. She almost threw it in the pile of rubbish. Of what use were a lot of old stamps? But something made her put it aside to save.

A year went by before she thought of it again. The house had been sold. "Nothing had happened." She was bitter. Her prayer had not been answered. Then one day she happened to see an advertisement in a large city newspaper, listing the value of certain rare stamps. Mrs. Horton made a special trip to see the dealer, carrying the old collection with her. When she left his office she was dazed and unbelieving, for in her purse she had his check for nearly $11,000!

The big old house had been much too large for one woman to care for comfortably. She did not need all that space. Today she realizes it. What she required was smaller living quarters together with enough money in the bank for her expenses. That is exactly what God gave her in answer to her supposedly "unanswered" prayer.

Then there was the businessman who had been praying for an increase in salary. Instead his company reshuffled its personnel and he was placed in a different department with a pay *decrease*. They told him he could leave if he was not satisfied to stay on at the lower figure.

He phoned me about the new development and his voice was bitter. "What good is prayer?" he demanded. This is just another variation on the "But nothing happened" theme. Where was God in all this, he wanted to know. Where indeed? Right where He always is, of course, busy making all things work together for good in our individual lives. Had nothing happened?

It seems that my friend had never before been engaged in

selling but the new job gave him a chance to try his hand at it and he proved to have a genius for it. Today, three years later, he is sales manager for his firm at a salary five times larger than the one he was receiving when he first prayed for an increase. More important still, he is doing work that is productive and rewarding. Had he not been "demoted," the promotion could never have happened.

My final story concerns a very dear neighbor whose retarded child could not seem to learn. Betty came to me in great distress one day. "It's the last straw," she burst. "As if I didn't already have enough grief and trouble with poor little Karen, now I have to take in my husband's father. He's practically senile. Oh please pray as you never prayed before that we can get some other relative to take care of him."

But there was no other relative able to take in the old man. The day Grandpa arrived my neighbor echoed the same old sad refrain, "We prayed, but nothing happened. I'm stuck." Nothing happened? It looked that way, didn't it? But God had something wonderful in store for that mother. He had the highest welfare of her retarded child at heart. For tiny Karen began to blossom in Grandpa's company. They seemed to understand each other and soon they were inseparable. Grandpa was not critical of her failings and never pushed her beyond her capacity. He accepted and loved her as she was and for herself alone.

For hours on end Karen sat in Grandpa's lap while he rocked and sang to her. She began to talk and laugh and play. Today she is a practically normal child and although the old man now is no longer living, the family is eternally grateful that God brought him to stay with them and love Karen into overcoming her handicap.

Make no mistake, there is no such thing as an unanswered prayer. God hears every whisper of our hearts but He loves us too much always to answer in the precise terms that we ask. He often has a better answer.

So never say "but nothing happened" when your prayers are not immediately fulfilled as you think they should be. Something always happens. A spiritual force has been set in motion that never stops vibrating in the universal atmosphere. A great chain reaction takes place which may not bring you exactly what you asked for, perhaps, but something infinitely better for your eternal advantage. In short, it is impossible for you to pray and then be able to say truthfully, "But nothing happened."

The Box

MARY LOUISE KITSEN

"There's more to do than I can handle," I said loudly and clearly. Of course, there was no one to hear my complaint except the three cats lying on the bed. Two of them continued sleeping while the third laid her ears back and switched her tail.

I sighed. There were writing assignments to be done (I'm a full-time freelance writer), my cousins were coming from Kansas in a few days and I felt I had to clean the entire house. And my mother was in the hospital again, which meant two trips there each day. How would I get to everything?

Deciding that Jesus was the only One who was listening, I addressed Him directly this time. "With Your help, I'll make it, but please, don't let anything else happen right now."

It was still early in the morning. I slipped my robe on and started downstairs. Maybe if I relaxed briefly with some toast and coffee, taking a look at the morning paper at the same time, I'd feel ready to tackle the busy day ahead. I opened the door and picked up the newspaper. Then I saw the box.

Where did it come from? It was a large box with "Corn-Flakes" written on the side. An old, rusted window screen lay on top; a rope kept it in place. Oh, no . . . someone who knows how I feel about cats must have dumped some kittens on me again. Just what I needed!

I started to pick the box up, and when I felt how heavy it was, I thought. "They've dumped the mother cat too." Actually, I didn't know the half of it!

I set the box down in the living room, untied the rope and looked in. There was a big yellow cat. But where were her kittens? I reached in and lifted the cat out. It started to purr immediately and pushed its head tightly against my shoulder. One big cat? A male at that.

I held the cat up to take a better look at him. And started to sob. This big, beautiful cat had no eyes—just white skin where his eyes should have been. I cradled him as my other cats started to gather. Pip-Squeak rubbed against the newcomer with evident pleasure. But what was I going to do with a blind kitty? How much care would he need?

I looked in the box to see if there was anything else and found the note: "This is Poppy. My dad hates having him around and said he'd shoot him if Mom and I didn't get rid of him ourselves. Please take care of him." It was in the handwriting of a youngster. Poor, sad child trying to keep a blind cat alive.

Poppy ate with the other cats—to my surprise and relief—and I showed him the litter box. I got absolutely nothing done before it was time to leave for the hospital; and I worried about leaving the cat in a strange place. But he seemed content and interested in investigating things. I called the vet's office and made an appointment. Then I left, praying that Poppy would make out all right.

When I returned home, I found Poppy sleeping with Pip-Squeak in the sunny dining room window. In the early afternoon I put him in a carrier and headed for the vet's office. I hated to take him, but I had to have help in this matter. The vet took him into a back room to check him over. I sat straight as a pin, not knowing what to expect.

The vet finally came out. He was alone. My heart did a flip-flop. What about Poppy? At that moment I realized the big yellow cat had stolen my heart.

"Someone took good care of that fellow," the doctor told me. "He's in good shape and amazingly contented. We'll keep him a couple days. He should be altered and have some shots, and there are a few tests we'd like to do."

I grinned.

Then the bomb fell. "We think Poppy is deaf and dumb as well as blind."

For the next two days I wondered how I'd manage a pet that couldn't see, hear or make a sound. I prayed about the cat. And, to my surprise, I was getting an awful lot of things accomplished even though my mind stayed on Poppy. It was as though Poppy was a challenge and so everything else was a challenge too.

I brought Poppy and my mother home from their respective hospitals just two days later. I went for Mom first and got her settled in her favorite chair in the living room. Then I went for Poppy.

Mom moved to the edge of her chair as I brought the carrier in. I opened it and Poppy climbed into my arms. How he loved people! I carried him over to Mom and she gathered him to her. In minutes, Poppy purred happily on her lap. It was the start of a warm, personal friendship between an elderly lady and a handicapped kitty cat—a relationship that has made both of their lives happier.

Poppy had helped me too. I was feeling sorry for myself when he came, but through him I gained a better attitude. It seemed almost as if Jesus had helped guide Poppy's owners to the act of bringing him to me. Little by little I began to think more and more about the mother and child who had left Poppy in my care. Who were they? Would they wonder about what had happened to Poppy?

And then one day I made a sign that said "Poppy is fine" and taped it to my front porch. I hoped the youngster who had brought the cat to me would see it.

The sign stayed up for several days. Then came the morning I went outside to the garage and I saw something that made my life even better. Written on the bottom of the sign I'd made were two messages, evidently written by the child and his mother—or that's what I've always thought. The child's writing said, "Thank you." The adult's hand wrote, "God Bless You."

I Asked for Bread

AUTHOR UNKNOWN

I asked for bread; God gave a stone instead.
Yet, while I pillowed there my weary head,
The angels made a ladder of my dreams,
Which upward to celestial mountains led.
And when I woke beneath the morning's beams,
Around my resting place fresh manna lay;
And, praising God, I went upon my way.
    For I was fed.

God answers prayer; sometimes when hearts are weak,
He gives the very gifts believers seek.
But often faith must learn a deeper rest,
And trust God's silence when He does not speak;
For He whose name is Love will send the best.
Stars may burn out, nor mountain walls endure,
But God is true, His promises are sure
    For those who seek.

First Year of Teaching

SARAH BRADFORD*

I looked at the blond teenager slumped at his desk in the back row of my classroom and felt sick inside.

Only six weeks ago, before I started my first year of teaching English to college freshmen, I had prayed, "God, please send me students who need what I can give." And now I asked despairingly, "Why, Lord? Why did You send me Robby?"

There was absolutely nothing I could give this student. I suspected strongly that he was an alcoholic, and that was a disease I'd had no luck coping with.

When I stopped at his desk to return a paper he'd handed in, it was clear that he'd been drinking before class. Once again he smelled like a brewery; his eyes were bloodshot; his hair, disheveled. My words tumbled out before I could stop them. "Robby, are you in the habit of drinking beer for breakfast?"

I regretted the sarcasm but couldn't control my frustration. I felt as angry and helpless as I had been on a Christmas Eve during my childhood when my father staggered into the tree on his way to the kitchen for another beer. Ornaments shattered on the hardwood floor, and the colored lights sputtered and went out. After my mother helped him up, he still got that beer. "Mama, don't you ever want to g-give up?" I asked in an unsteady voice. She sighed. "He needs me to stand by him and pray for him. With God's help, somehow, someway . . . well, I know he'll find his way."

Now, in my classroom, Robby looked at his desk and shoved both hands into the pockets of his jeans. "I'm rushing a fraternity," he muttered. "You must smell beer from the party last night."

I shook my head. "Robby, you've already missed three classes." I held out the theme he'd written. "And a D on your first paper isn't a good way to start the semester."

He looked up pleadingly. "But I won't be absent anymore. I promise. And I'll work harder on my next paper."

Classes were changing, and before I could respond, he had risen and disappeared into the crowd. I walked briskly down the

---

*Names have been changed.

hall to my office. I hated myself for being angry and blamed
Robby for making me feel that way.

He's just like my father, I thought. He was unreachable. Irresponsible. How many times had I tried to get through to my
father—to no avail? And then more heartbreak—my younger
brother started drinking. Again and again I'd begged him to stop,
bailed him out of jail, listened to his lame excuses. All for nothing. My heels drummed on the terrazzo floor of the hall. Robby
would have to solve his own problems, I decided. I had nothing
left to give.

For the next several weeks, Robby did come to class regularly.
Slumping at a desk in the back left-hand corner of my classroom,
he daydreamed or gazed out the window into bright leaves and
sunshine. Sometimes he'd get up during a class discussion to go
outside and drink from the water fountain.

The two papers he handed in looked as if they'd been dashed
off. I marked a large D on each. Yet when I lectured or led
discussions, I'd find myself looking back to Robby's corner of
the classroom. His eyes carefully avoided my gaze; sometimes
he'd flinch, as if recoiling from a punch.

When I handed back Robby's fourth assignment, I watched
him open it to the back page. His eyes fell on the inevitable D,
and I saw tears well in his eyes.

They always cry, I thought bitterly, remembering how my father's large hands would shake as he'd cover his face and say he
was sorry and promise to change. Now, for some reason, I felt
guilty, as if I were the cause of Robby's misery. I quickly caught
myself. I would not be manipulated into feeling responsible.
"He's got to take responsibility," I vowed.

Determined to confront him, I caught him at the door after
class. "Robby, can we talk a minute?" I asked. He looked at the
floor and didn't answer. "I—I don't like giving D's," I began,
"but you haven't given me much choice."

"I can't write like you want," he muttered. "Whatever it is
you want, I can't do it."

I stiffened. *That's always it,* I thought. Blame anything but the
alcohol. Just give up. Expect to be bailed out. "Robby, you could
write perfectly well," I found myself saying, "if you'd stop drinking and start caring about your work."

He looked up at me. "I hate the paper topics," he countered.
"They're stupid."

Paper topics were under the control of the English Department and I assigned what the syllabus demanded. Now Robby wanted me to make an exception for him. I hated exceptions. I stared at Robby; for a fleeting moment I recalled my mother's eyes, warm and steady, reflecting her conviction. I could hear her saying firmly, "We won't give up on your father. We'll go on believing that God can give him the will to change." Something broke within me—or maybe I was just tired of being angry, unsure of what to do next. I knew what Mama would do.

Robby poked nervously at a hole in his faded jeans, shuffled his feet and waited for me to respond. Then, obviously anxious to retreat, he tried to edge past me. "It's not your problem," he said. "You can just flunk me and forget it."

But I stood there blocking his path. He was wrong. It *was* my problem. I remembered the prayer I'd said before school began. I hadn't asked God for the best students but for those who needed what I could give.

I took a deep breath. "Okay, Robby, on the next paper you can write about anything you want. Forget the assignment sheet. Just make sure your paper's at least two full pages, and . . . and that it's about something that matters to you."

His eyes widened in disbelief. "Anything?" he asked.

"*Anything,*" I answered.

Afterward I worried that I'd violated the letter of the law set down by the English Department for freshman composition. But I consoled myself by arguing that I hadn't violated its spirit. I went on worrying about Robby and my response to him while I cooked dinner, did my laundry and fed the cat. A week later, after he handed in his next paper, I pulled it from the pile as soon as I sat down in my office, anxious to discover what he had to say. Neatly stapled together were six full pages of small, careful print. The first sentences were: "Kevin woke up with his face in the high grass beside the interstate. He could hear cars whizzing by and his head hurt. He'd blacked out again."

I looked up from the paper and felt my eyes begin to sting. Taking a long gulp of coffee, I kept reading. In a moving, concrete and straightforward style, Robby continued for six pages describing the life of a teenage alcoholic. "Kevin," he wrote, "hated looking into the mirror at himself. It made him want another beer." The Kevin that Robby described lost friends because of his drinking, woke up in places he couldn't remember arriving at, and made D's in chemistry, calculus and English. He felt "desperate, alone and sure of dying."

At his paper's conclusion, Robby added a postscript: "Miss Bradford, this is not me. I wanted to try writing fiction, but I don't want you to think this is me." I pushed his paper aside, put my head on my desk and cried. All of the times my father had bellowed, "I don't have a drinking problem," replayed themselves on the screen of my thoughts.

I reached for a tissue. What should I do? If I referred Robby to the alcohol treatment program at Student Services, he wouldn't go. If I contacted his counselor at the General College, what would I say? That to every alcoholic his dependency is only fiction? That I had a way of knowing when people drank too much? That I'd grown up with an alcoholic father? That my younger brother had looked just like Robby his first year in college—the year he wrecked two cars and nearly killed himself? I knew I wasn't a counselor, a social worker or a psychiatrist, and I was sure Robby's presence in my class had been some kind of cosmic mistake. *I'm just an English teacher,* I thought. But the words stuck in my mind as if they contained the answer. *You are an English teacher. Just teach English the very best way you can.*

I poured another cup of coffee. Then, with an almost peaceful determination, I began grading the paper. Scrupulously I marked every misspelling or grammatical error, put in absent commas and suggested shorter paragraphs. Finally, in my end note I wrote, "Robby, this is your best paper yet. Concrete, compelling and interesting. You involve the reader in Kevin's painful, desperate situation. But fiction requires a conclusion. What happens to Kevin? Does he find help or end up a victim of the bottle? For your next paper, I'd like you to finish the story." I scrawled a large B below the note.

When I handed the papers back, Robby was in class, but he missed the two classes that followed. Panic crept over me at odd moments that week. Had I done something so wrong that he'd decided not to come back at all? How could I have imagined I could help such a confused, haunted teenager? I knew if he didn't show up for class the next time, I'd have to notify his adviser.

When I walked into my classroom on Monday morning, I immediately looked back at Robby's seat. It was empty. As I opened my book, I tried to squelch disappointment long enough to teach the other students.

Then, glancing up to take roll, my heart jumped. Robby was there after all, but not in his usual seat in the corner. He'd moved to the second row. His hair was combed, and he wore a bright-green polo shirt and crisp khaki pants. I'd never seen him in anything but torn jeans and an old shirt. Catching my gaze, he smiled broadly.

Back in my office an hour later I turned to the conclusion of Robby's "fictitious" narrative. He'd written a single paragraph: "I couldn't write it. I was afraid how it would end up. I'm not drinking anymore and I'm going to Alcoholics Anonymous.* I know I can finish this now—if I can just get an extension."

I wrote at the bottom of the sheet, "Extension granted."

I still saw Robby after he finished my class, taking away a B— as his course grade. Usually it was early in the morning. I'd be walking across campus, clutching a cup of coffee, not yet awake, and I'd hear him shouting exuberantly, "Hey, Miss Bradford, how's it goin'?"

Robby had needed the professionals he went looking for and found. But I'd been wrong in arrogantly declaring that I had nothing to give. He'd needed me to believe he could make the changes so important to his leading a healthy, productive life. My mother had been that believing person for my father and brother—to this day faithful members of Alcoholics Anonymous.

I thank God for using my classroom as one of the instruments in Robby's change. And I remember Robby at the beginning of each semester when I carefully pray, "God, send me students who need what I can give."

A Prayer, a Pledge and a Promise

JO GARDNER

I'd tossed and turned that Saturday night, unable to sleep. Part of the trouble was that my husband, Jim, and I were living in our

---

*If you want to know more about A.A., write to P.O. Box 459, Grand Central Station, New York, NY 10163, or look for the phone number listed in your local directory's white pages under A.A.

daughter's house. The catering business we'd sunk everything into had failed. While we were getting back on our feet financially, Vicki had welcomed us into her home, but I felt uneasy about being there. And then too, I kept thinking about the meeting I had said I'd attend at church the next day.

Our new sanctuary was under construction that spring, yet not all the money to pay for it had been raised. I knew the elders would be calling for pledges at the meeting, and I hated that we had nothing to give. Strangely, as I lay there staring at the ceiling, the figure of $1,000 had flashed through my head—not once, but several times. It was so preposterous I'd almost laughed. A thousand dollars. Imagine my pledging a thousand dollars!

The next day at the meeting in the fellowship hall of Escondido's Cathedral of the Valley, I hung my head and offered my apologies to God as I heard pledges being called out all around me. And, as I sat there, once more the figure of $1,000 danced strangely in my head.

Lord, I prayed, if we had it, I'd give it to You.

You can earn it, came the answer in my head.

But how? I asked. I'm just a wife and mother. I have no training, no job, no money-making prospects.

You have a talent.

No, Lord, I think the only thing I've ever done well is make quilts.

Then make Me a quilt. His words were even more distinct than the voices in the fellowship hall.

Before I knew what I was doing, I was on my feet saying stoutly, "I'll make a quilt! I know this is unusual, but I'll make a quilt and sell it, and whatever I get for it will go to the building fund."

"What do you think your quilt will bring?" someone asked.

"Four hundred, maybe five hundred dollars," I blurted.

"Who will give this lady five hundred dollars for her quilt?" the leader asked.

Across the room a woman named Lee Clarke, whom I knew faintly, stood up. "I'll give her five hundred dollars for it," she said.

"Oh, my goodness," I mumbled. It was dizzying. God had directed me to pledge a quilt, and now He had supplied a buyer.

I sank down in my seat, bowed my head and promised God that only my very best work would be done on His quilt.

The meeting buzzed on around me. Others were now making offers of services as well as cash. Then I heard a voice above all the others say, "I think that quilt is worth a thousand dollars, and I'll give that."

I sprang to my feet. It was Lee Clarke again. She had raised her own bid! But how could that be? No one had bid against her, and how could she have known about the figure in my head?

As soon as the meeting was over, I rushed up to Lee. "Thank you, but one thousand dollars is a lot to pay for a quilt," I told her.

"Don't worry," she said breezily. "They probably get that and more over in those shops in Rancho Santa Fe."

Strange, I thought, *if Lee hadn't offered to buy it, I was going to sell it myself to one of those shops.* We made a date to discuss patterns and colors, and I left, half in wonderment, half in jubilation.

Lee selected a lovely open-fan design and chose colors of brown, cream and gold. As soon as Jim and I were able to relocate into our own house, I began quilting in earnest, working eight hours a day, three to five days a week. The work was going well, but the project was so enormous that sometimes it overwhelmed me.

During these times I often turned to prayer. I prayed for patience so that the quilt would be as near perfect as I could make it. As I stitched I asked God to be with all those who would use His quilt. I began to form a picture of a woman holding the quilt, cherishing it, and I prayed for her too.

The winter months melted together. By March I had all the patchwork pieced together, and I began lining the quilt. On March 15, 1984, I embroidered my name and the date on an upper corner of the lining. "It is finished, Lord," I said. "Let this quilt be a blessing to our church, and bless the home it goes into with peace and security."

The following Sunday, I gave the quilt to Lee. I asked her to hold one corner of it so I could open it up to full size.

"Oh," she whispered, "it's beautiful. It must have a million stitches in it." She didn't say much more, but she couldn't seem to take her eyes off it. I believed she was pleased with it, and I was happy because $1,000 had been added to my church's building fund.

Two months later, on an afternoon in May, I was returning from an errand when I spotted Lee on our front porch. She had the quilt in her arms.

"Is something the matter?" I asked her.

"Jo," she blurted, "I have to give this back to you."

I was stunned. "What's wrong with it?"

"I love it," she said softly, "but I cannot keep it. . . . I have a feeling about it I can't explain. There is so much of you in it. Jo, this is *your* quilt. Please take it."

She pressed it into my hands.

"Jo," she said, "there is just one stipulation I want to make. Don't ever let this beautiful thing get out of your family. It must be part of your family's heritage."

"God bless you," I said. "Oh, Jo, God bless you." Then she was gone, and I was sitting on the sofa, pressing the quilt to my chest. I had made many quilts, but never had I kept one for myself. Now God had given back to me the very quilt I had made for Him.

And then it came to me: The woman I had prayed for, the one I had pictured in my prayers—that woman was me. And the home I had asked God to bless with peace and security, that was my home, Jim's and mine. Truly our God is amazing. Just as the Bible verse promises: "Give, and it shall be given unto you; good measure, pressed down, and shaken together, and running over" (Luke 6:38).

Running over, like the quilt I held on my lap, turning gold in the late afternoon sun.

Conclusion

The Mercy Prayer

Lord Jesus Christ, have mercy on me.

A Short Form

MERYLL M. HESS

A friend told me that the Greek Orthodox have a prayer that goes "Lord Jesus, have mercy on me a miserable sinner." Someone realized that God already knew he was miserable, so he dropped that word, leaving "Lord Jesus, have mercy on me a sinner." Then he decided God certainly knew he was a sinner, so that was dropped. The editing continued until only one word was left: "Jesus!"

As a busy wife and mother of four, I have found many exciting uses for that prayer, while driving, cooking, answering children's questions. It adds hours of prayer to each hectic day.

The Mercy Prayer

CATHERINE MARSHALL

During a telephone chat, my friend Elaine was telling me about a christening she had just attended. "The baby being christened was not only crying but screaming," she said. "I could see how embarrassed the infant's parents were and I wanted to help them. So I prayed, 'Lord Jesus, have mercy on that baby and his father and mother.'

"Catherine, it was remarkable. The crying stopped immediately as if a faucet had been turned off."

I agreed that it was amazing, then added, "But, Elaine, the result doesn't surprise me as much as your particular petition."

"How so?"

"Oh, just that the 'have mercy' seems such an extreme request in a relatively mild situation. Most of us think of mercy as connected with a dire emergency. The word conjures up a mental picture of a condemned man standing before a judge pleading for pity."

Then Elaine explained how it had indeed been a dire emergency that had begun to reveal to her the many facets of God's mercy . . .

Eight years before, her husband Louis had undergone a serious cancer operation. He recovered and had been in good health until last summer when his doctor suspected a return of the cancer. "It was a time of great agony," Elaine told me. "All my reading of Scripture and praying—hours of it—led to a fresh realization of the unceasing compassion of a God of love.

"So my praying," she went on, "finally jelled into a single, heartfelt plea, 'Father in Heaven, will You have mercy on us simply for Jesus' sake?' "

The result? The cancer scare proved to be a false alarm.

But then Elaine went on to explain that, since then, God keeps showing her how He wants us to ask for and accept His mercy even in everyday things.

In the next few days, it was remarkable how passage after passage of Scripture verifying Elaine's Mercy Prayer was brought to my attention. I saw that many of Jesus' healings came as the result of a plea for mercy.

For instance, there were the two blind men sitting by the side of the road as Jesus was leaving Jericho (Matthew 20:29–34). Hearing that this was Jesus passing by, the two men cried out, "Have mercy on us, O Lord, thou son of David."

The crowd following the Master told them to keep quiet. But the blind men cried the louder, "Have mercy on us."

And Jesus, standing still and giving the men His full attention, asked what they wanted of Him. When they begged Jesus to open their eyes, *He had compassion on them*, touched the eyes of both men, and immediately each received his sight.

Then there was the time Jesus met ten lepers (Luke 17:11–19). Since lepers were ostracized from public gatherings, these men stood at a distance, crying, "Jesus, Master, have mercy on us."

The Master did not question each man about how well he had kept the Law or how righteous he was. Simply out of Jesus' overflowing, compassionate love, He healed them. "Go and show yourselves to the priests," He told them. And later, "Your faith has restored you to health" (The Amplified Bible).

Faith in what or in whom? The connecting link is our belief that God loves each of us with a love more wondrous than the most warmhearted person we know; that He heals simply out of His love and because He wants us to have the joy of abundant health. As the Apostle Paul put it: "Blessed be the God and Father of our Lord Jesus Christ, the Father of mercies and God of all comfort, who comforts us in all our affliction" (2 Corinthians 1:3, 4, RSV).

In another place Paul tells us why Jesus did not inquire about the worthiness of those whom He healed or lifted out of sin: "So then (God's gift) is not a question of human will and human effort, but of God's mercy . . ." (Romans 9:16, Amplified). In other words, there is nothing you or I can do to earn God's gifts. We are dependent on His loving mercy.

When I searched out the word *mercy* in Cruden's *Concordance*, I found a surprisingly long list of Scripture references. Moreover, Alexander Cruden's original words of description set down in 1769 are rich food for thought: "Mercy signifies that essential perfection in God, whereby He pities and relieves the miseries of His creatures"; and " 'Grace' flows from 'mercy' as its fountain."

The insights about the Mercy Prayer were not over yet. During a wakeful time in the middle of the next night, the inner Voice (there is no mistaking it!) forcibly reminded me of the particular words of the promise God had given me on the morning of Peter Marshall's death back in 1949. It had come as I had been about to leave the hospital room in which my husband's body lay. Even as I had reached for the doorknob, it was as if a firm hand had stopped me. Then, clearly and emphatically, yet with tenderness combined with surprising power, had come, "Goodness and mercy shall follow you all the days of your life."

And now, so many years later, deep in the night, the same Voice was saying, "Note that word 'mercy,' Catherine. My goodness, My mercy. That's what is following you and will surround you to the end of your earthly walk. Lean back on that. Depend on it."

How needed that assurance was for me at a particular moment thirty-three years ago. How needed for anyone in distress!

For who among us does not have needs in our troubled age? And to meet those needs, the resounding validity of the Mercy Prayer all through Scripture is meant for every one of us . . . "The Lord is good; his *mercy* is everlasting; and his truth endureth to all generations" (Psalm 100:5, *italics added*).

Prayer

BOOK OF COMMON PRAYER, 1928

O Lord,
support us all the day long,
until the shadows lengthen and the evening comes,
and the busy world is hushed.
Then in Thy mercy grant us a safe lodging,
and a holy rest,
and peace at the last.